365 GAMES
TODDLERS PLAY

365 GAMES TODDLERS PLAY

Creative Time to Imagine, Grow and Learn

Sheila Ellison
Bestselling author of
365 DAYS OF CREATIVE PLAY

SOURCEBOOKS, INC.®
NAPERVILLE, ILLINOIS

Published by Sourcebooks, Inc.
P.O. Box 4410, Naperville, Illinois 60567-4410
(630) 961-3900
FAX: (630) 961-2168
www.sourcebooks.com

Library of Congress Cataloging-in-Publication Data

Ellison, Sheila.
  365 games toddlers play / by Sheila Ellison.
      p. cm.
  ISBN 1-4022-0176-1 (alk. paper)
  1. Toddlers—Development. 2. Child development. 3. Play. 4. Parent
and child. 5. Parenting. I. Title: Three hundred sixty five games
toddlers play. II. Title.
HQ774.5.E45 2003
649'.55—dc21
                              2003005851

Printed and bound in the United States of America
VP 10 9 8 7 6 5 4 3 2 1

Acknowledgment

To Alisa Ikeda, for the creative contribution of activities, ideas, and enthusiasm she poured into this book. Alisa is a writer, certified instructor of infant massage, wife, and proud mother of two, Sawyer and Sadie. She lives in Marin County, California. She's an active member of Mothers and More as well as an advocate for public policies that are mother-, child-, and family-friendly. Alisa holds a BA in sociology and writes regularly about parenting, family, and social issues.

Dedication

To my children, Wesley, Brooke, Rhett, and Troy for proving that my parenting theories—which began as experiments on them when they were toddlers—actually work!

Introduction

Life is a game for toddlers. Everything everywhere calls out to be touched, manipulated, jumped on, tasted, and examined. Being a young explorer is serious business—learning, testing, and pushing the limits to see just how much you can get away with before somebody notices—and it takes a lot of energy! Toddlers are thrilled when parents aren't afraid to get down on the floor with them; plunge their hands into the mud, paint, or dough; dance wildly to homemade instruments; or put on a silly puppet show. Toddler time is full of wonder, interaction, explaining, setting limits, and teaching social skills. It is also a time for parents to learn a great deal about how exciting and new the world can be when experienced from a toddler's perspective. So dive in. Use the activities on the following pages to have fun with your toddler. Don't be afraid to wander off the beaten path into new territory; draw outside the lines, use your imagination, make up your own variation to an activity as you encourage self-expression. It is in the everyday moments that life happens—so make those moments special.

Words of Wisdom

The advice in the Words of Wisdom sections of this book was given to us by parents from across the country who wanted to pass on their tricks, tips, toddler secrets, and wisdom to you. We would like to thank them for sharing their experiences with us. We're always looking for good advice to be added to future editions, so write to us care of Sourcebooks or visit Sheila Ellison at www.CompleteMom.com.

Table of Contents

Section One:
Day-to-Day Life

Toddler Survival Tips

Parent-to-Parent Bonding

Having kids might distance you from friends without kids. But it can automatically connect you to all the other parents out there. You've joined a club, so take advantage of membership benefits: swap tips on child-rearing, kid-friendly hot spots, shopping deals, movies and restaurants for twosome time, and even baby-sitter referrals. Laugh and cry with other moms and dads as bleary-eyed and deliriously happy as yourselves. So next time you see another parent with young children in the local bookstore, use your easy ice-breakers—your charming children— to strike up a conversation. It may well lead to a lasting friendship. Making an effort to connect with other parents will help you along this journey of raising great kids.

1

Stay Safe

Brush up on your CPR, especially if you only took infant CPR—the procedures change when Baby turns one! Post first-aid diagrams or instructions someplace you can see them immediately, like the inside of a kitchen cabinet. You childproofed for Baby, but now it's time to childproof for your curious and mobile toddler—look higher and think more creatively about the troubles he could find.

* Never leave your child around standing water alone, including the bathtub and toilet.
* Don't cook on the stovetop or in the oven with your child in your arms.
* Don't carry a child while holding hot food or drink.
* Invest in stove knob covers, and always keep pot handles facing in.
* Use the child safety locks on the car door, and make sure to have your car-seat installation inspected by a local highway patrol.
* Keep the crib drop side in the highest position.
* Don't forget the doorstops or protectors, window locks, sliding door locks, belts on shopping carts, and smoke detectors in every bedroom and in halls. Keep irons, curling irons, and knives out of reach, tether your furniture to the wall, and keep phone numbers for poison control and the police and fire departments handy. Mark sliding doors with colorful stickers, and make sure your child's bed is placed away from windows.

Just the Two of You

- Institute a regular and predictable date night, maybe once or twice a month. Make a rule for the night—no talking about the kids. If finances are an issue, find another couple who is willing to swap baby-sitting duties.
- Shower together whenever you can.
- Remember the art of flirting—in person, on the phone, by email, or whenever.
- Go to bed at the same time.
- Even if you're in a hurry don't forget a lingering kiss upon parting and reconnecting.
- Start a dream file together of all the things you'd each like to do in your life. Having children changes a couple's life; sometimes it helps to remember that there will be plenty of time to create and experience new dreams and adventures.

3

Time for Self

For parents of toddlers, this might be the most important survival tip!

- Schedule a regular, predictable getaway. Take a class or get a gym membership where childcare is free.
- Girls' or Guys' Night Out: don't forget to nurture your friendships. Take turns watching the kids so that you each get a night out with friends.
- Add ritual to your days. Start each morning with a slowly steeped cup of tea in a beautiful cup and saucer with a cookie or biscuit. Sip and eat slowly. Or start each evening with a glass of wine or sparkling cider and a few crackers, pieces of cheese, and apples or grapes. Prepare them purposefully, and savor each flavor and texture.
- Nourish a hobby that's all your own. If you like to read, join or start a reading group. If you want to try your hand at knitting, sign up for a local class.
- Go outside every day, walk around, breathe deeply, and be thankful.
- Order a magazine that has nothing to do with your work or your family and everything to do with you and your individual interests. Then be sure to give yourself the time to read it cover to cover before the next issue arrives.
- Create a sanctuary. Find an inviting space in your home—a bathroom, a corner of the bedroom, a breakfast nook, a side table and chair in the living room—and claim it as a kid-free zone. Make it beautiful and personal and escape there whenever you can. Consider adding a basket of books or magazines, a candle, and a CD player with a stack of your favorite music.

4

Balancing Work with Home

- When you return from work, have a timer by the door and set it for ten "decompression" minutes. Make a rule that no one can bug you 'til it beeps.
- Take a sick day—sometimes being sick is the only way off of the treadmill and the only way to energize yourself.
- Both Mom and Dad are tired and overworked. If possible, stop the bickering and start delegating. Consider hiring a housecleaner once a month, schedule a regular take-out night so nobody has to cook, or put the kids in bed an hour early a few nights a week.
- Make a list of nonnegotiable things that must get done regularly: dishes, laundry, cooking, taking out the garbage—and decide how to divvy them up. The key is assigning tasks in advance, when no one is angry.
- Every couple of weeks, when everything is starting to feel out of control, set aside one morning, evening, or day to catch up on the bigger tasks like bill-paying, vacuuming, or scrubbing showers. Play great music, and work together to make it less of a chore and more of an event.

5

Coping with a Toddler's Energy

Even the most energetic of parents gets tired out by a toddler's endless curiosity, movement, and energy—here are a few things you can try.

* Institute a regular quiet time every day.
* Hire mommy's helper—a local teen, perhaps—to play with your child periodically while you're home and trying to cook dinner.
* Set aside a time for active play every day—preferably outdoors where there are sun and wind to wear them out even further!
* Be a calming force. Don't let them wind you up. Whenever you feel overwhelmed, just sit down and take a breather. Sometimes our toddlers get going so fast because they watch us trying to do too much at one time. Stay calm, and they'll follow your lead.

6

Clutter Cutters

Tired of a house full of toys? Clear the clutter without a tinge of guilt.

- Set up a standard cleaning time each day. Make up your own clean-up song and have your kids pitch in.
- Make an effort to have plenty of storage containers so that everything has a home. Give away everything you don't have space for.
- Rotate the toys so they're not all out at once. Decide on one place in the house, possibly the garage or basement, where clutter is welcome.
- Establish a routine whereby only one project is out at a time.
- Create toy-free zones where no children's toys or projects are allowed.

7

Stop-the-Whining Tips

- Make clear to your child what whining is—imitate (and exaggerate) the tone. When she whines, act like it's painful: act horrified, furrow your brow, or cover your ears.
- Pretend that you can't hear her or understand her words. Tell her you can't respond to her request until she talks normally.
- Suggest she whine elsewhere. Some parents use a "whining chair" or room. Allow her to come back to you when she's ready to talk nicely.
- Set a timer that marks the amount of time she's allowed to whine. When the timer goes off, ask her to come back and ask again without the whine.
- Give a focused answer when you sense a whine is on the horizon. Bend down on a knee and look her directly in the eye when you tell her whatever it is you have to say. If you're distracted, busy, or vague, the whine seems to grow.
- Respond readily to the pleasant requests; let her know that nice voices are heard and that whining doesn't produce results.
- Be consistent at home and in public.

8

Taming the Tantrum

* Videotape the tantrum as it's happening. This will make your child self-conscious, and later you can show it to him. Seeing how silly he looks might deter him from doing it again.
* If you have no camera available, use a hand-held mirror. Place it in front of him so he can watch how his face is changing. He may get so interested in watching himself that he forgets whatever he was tantruming over.
* Gently but firmly hold him and comfort him. Sing a song with a soothing rhythm and distracting lyrics.
* Stay calm, continue doing what you are doing, and ignore the tantrum completely.
* Throw your own tantrum—the spectacle may be enough to snap him out of it.
* Offer choices to avoid the tantrum. If he throws a fit at getting dressed, let him choose the outfit from two or three options.
* Give adequate warning time for activity changes. "We're leaving the park in five minutes…now four minutes…"

Choosing a Daycare or Preschool

* Do some soul-searching about how exactly you want this to enrich your child's life. Do you want a homey atmosphere, structure, academics, or a mix of this and that? What about the presence or use of computers or television? What's the curriculum? How does it evolve over the week, month, or year? Once you figure out what you want for your child, you'll know what to look for, and you'll recognize it when you see it.
* Consider the teacher-child ratio, gender balance, staff training, background, length of service with the school, turnover rate, parent participation, toilet-training requirements or procedures, and sick policies for children and staff. Who fills in for absent teachers? How often are toys cleaned? What is the appearance of the bathrooms and kitchen?
* Bring a partner or a friend so you can both ask questions and form opinions independently. Talk about the pros and cons afterward.
* Look for a place with teachers or directors whose philosophies mesh with your own—a place that disciplines and comforts much like you do at home.
* Watch how the teachers or directors handle things that arise during your visit.
* Word of mouth is important, but trust your instincts as well. And, most of all, get references from families who attend.

Baby-Sitter Tips

* When choosing a baby-sitter, consider age, experience, and personality. If you choose to go with a younger, less experienced, less expensive sitter, try to find a neighbor whose parent will be home and readily accessible any time the sitter is with your child. In any case, get references from other families.
* You might suggest and even coordinate and cover any expenses for baby-sitting training and CPR or first-aid classes.
* Have the sitter come for the interview, and then let the sitter play a little bit with your child while you are home. Listen to how she interacts with your child. If this is not possible, at least have the sitter arrive early so your child feels comfortable when you leave.
* Let your child pick out some games or activities in advance. That way he'll be excited about the sitter coming to play with him, and he'll know what to expect. You might also treat them to something special for dinner.
* Type and laminate a baby-sitters' guide. Include emergency numbers, cell phone numbers, a neighbor's phone number, discipline guidelines, food restrictions, the usual schedule or routine, and the family name, phone numbers, and address.
* If you are hiring a baby-sitter who has regular weekly hours, make sure to consider holiday bonuses as well as vacation time to express your appreciation.

11

Getting Things Done

* Make a game out of vacuuming the floor. Make it a race to see how fast the kids can clear your path of toys!
* When mopping the floor, turn your table chairs into a school bus—line them up one behind another so they look like bus seating. Sing "The Wheels on the Bus" while your child takes a seat and pretends to drive (and stays out of your way!).
* Take a leisurely shower. Instead of setting up your child outside the shower and praying he doesn't have a meltdown when the shampoo is still in your hair, bring him in with lots of plastic kitchen goods (measuring cups, pasta scoops, etc.) and let him enjoy the waterfall.
* Phone calls: devise a signal (a tap on your arm or something) so that your child can get your attention without verbally interrupting. Have a small activity box near the phone—easy, quiet things the child only does when you're going to be occupied on the phone for any length of time. The only rule is that he sits by you while he plays.
* Cooking: involve him in the easy stuff like stirring or pouring. Set up a cooking station for him with child-sized tools.
* Running errands: give him tasks to do like helping you look for grocery items or dropping mail in the mailbox.

12

Saying No

- Don't ask yes or no questions; instead, offer limited choices you can live with: "Would you like carrots or peas for your vegetable tonight?" or "What shall we put away first—the cars or the stuffed animals?" or "Do you want to go to bed now or in three minutes?" Then be firm.
- Also try changing "no" to "no, thank you"—it's far more tolerable!
- Sometimes there is no room for negotiation, and you simply say, "This is the way it is." Don't get upset—just be matter of fact.
- Try not to use the word "no" too often…she learns more by modeling than by anything else.
- Praise the "yes" answers endlessly! "It's so nice to hear you say 'yes'! Thank you. What a cooperative girl you are!"
- Set clear limits and give fair warnings. She needs to know what's expected of her and what the consequences will be.
- Choose your battles wisely. If something really doesn't matter to you, leave well enough alone.

13

Daily Routines

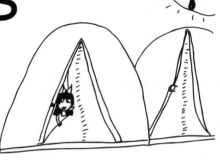

Daily Routine

Age Range: 15 months and up

A consistent daily schedule helps a child know what to expect, therefore creating fewer power struggles when moving from one part of the day to the next. It will also give parents a framework in their own day to do some of the things they'd like to do. Here's how to create a daily routine that works.

❀ For two or three days, write down what your child does naturally. For example, note if he is more energetic in the morning, likes to watch a show after lunch, or seems to fall asleep at a certain time.

❀ Think about your daily schedule. What are the things you need to get done in a day? When could you find time to relax?

❀ On a blank piece of paper draw seven boxes for the days of the week. Write into those boxes standing appointments.

❀ Next, looking at both your list and your child's, write down a schedule that combines both your needs and your child's needs. You don't need to write the specific activity you will be doing; it is enough to write arts and crafts, outdoors, resting, eating, preparing food, errands, or whatever else you need to fit into your schedule.

❀ Even with a schedule there will be days when things come up. Stay flexible!

14

Hand Washing Games

Age Range: 15 months and up

Toddlers seem to get their hands into everything. They sneeze, cough, pick things up off the floor, and touch everything they see. Here's how to teach them to wash their hands often and without constant reminder.

* Fill a tub with soapy water and place it on the kitchen counter. Put a toy in the bottom of the tub. Change the toy throughout the day so your child will wonder which toy is taking a bath. He will put his hands into the water to find the toy and get a hand washing at the same time. Make sure to put a towel next to the tub.

* Draw up a card that has a picture of hands under a water faucet. Whenever you serve food, put the card on the table on top of the food as a reminder to wash hands first. You won't have to say a word.

* Give a mini–hand massage as you wash your hands together: first you rub her hands and then she rubs yours.

....

Words of Wisdom: *My son began to brush his teeth with confidence when I bought a small mirror and put it on the edge of the bathroom counter. This way he can get right up close to it and see what he's doing.*

—Gloria, La Jolla, California

15

Good Morning

Age Range: 15 months and up

Sing a song: Start the day with a good-morning song. "Rise and Shine" or "You are My Sunshine" are good, upbeat choices. It will ease everyone into the day with a smile.

Wake up, tot: Start the day by playing a wake-up game. Say, "Wake up, hair!" and touch your toddler's hair gently. Then "Wake up, nose!" as you touch his nose, and on and on (chin, shoulders, knees) until you're eventually tickling his feet.

Stretch and greet: Once out of bed stretch as far up to the ceiling as you can to greet the sun. Then stretch forward to touch the ground. Stretch upwards again, then from side to side, greeting your day with energy and enthusiasm.

· ·

Words of Wisdom: *Sometimes I can't get off work to attend a function at my daughter's preschool, so I give the teacher an instant camera and ask her to take pictures. I get them developed right away so we can talk about the event.*

—Steven, Greenville, Michigan

16

Special Breaks

Go somewhere every day: A change of scenery rejuvenates us all, whether it's just a jaunt to the neighborhood park, the market, or an unexpected trip to a pet store, a neighbor's house, or the mall.

Nurture a hobby: Take your train-lover to the railroad tracks, your plane-lover to the airport, your budding artist to a children's museum.

Take a time out: When you, your toddler, or both of you are frustrated, stop and do something unexpected together—jump around to the count of twenty, shout out nonsense words, or pound on the floor.

Sit still: When you realize you're feeling stressed or harried, slow down to read a book together, share a glass of lemonade, or blow bubbles.

• •

WOrds of WisdOm: *My son can't stand getting haircuts. But once we made a superhero cape out of a plastic gift bag and let him wear goggles. With his new outfit the hair didn't itch his neck or get in his eyes, and he stopped complaining.*

—Laura, Spencerport, New York

17

Our Day

Age Range: 18 months and up

Take snapshots of a typical day in the life of your toddler: eating breakfast, doing laundry, playing with a friend, making lunch, building blocks, napping, greeting Mommy or Daddy after work, brushing teeth after dinner, etc. Once developed, glue them each to a separate piece of cardboard and attach a piece of Velcro to the back. Put a strip of poster board up on the wall with a self-adhesive strip of Velcro down the middle. Use the pictures to map out your child's day. Have her help you to stick them on the Velcro strip according to the day's schedule. If your child is in daycare, you might want to bring your camera and ask her caregivers to capture moments throughout her day. You can then add those pictures to the schedule board or use them to launch a discussion about her playmates and activities. This is a great way to stay connected, and it's a reminder of the fun she has at school to motivate her on those lazy, I-don't-want-to-go mornings. When you take the pictures, make sure to make duplicates; it is also fun to put the daily pictures into a travel-sized photo album that can travel anywhere with your child.

18

Dressing Fun

Age Range: 18 to 21 months

Sometimes toddlers develop a list of favorite clothes they like to wear. Often the favorites include costumes or clothes with big holes or stains, but they still want to wear them every day. Or maybe your child wants to wear a ballerina costume in the middle of winter. What can you do?

* When choosing clothes, give your child a few choices, like "Do you want to wear the blue sweater, the white sweatshirt, or the turtleneck?" Toddlers like to be in charge and will appreciate being given a choice.
* Take the warm-weather clothes and store them in a box during the winter. That way, you'll avoid an argument over bathing suits and shorts versus sweatpants.
* Teach your child how to put on her own jacket. Lay the jacket on the floor with the inside of the jacket facing up. Have her stand at the top of the jacket, bend down, and put her hands into the armholes. As she stands up, her jacket will flip over her head. Voila!
* Put together a box of clothes to be worn during messy projects.
* If you are staying home and don't care what your child wears, don't say a word; just get your camera ready.

19

Manners

Age Range: 24 months and up

Inside/outside voice: Start explaining early to your kids that everyone has two voices, an inside voice and an outside voice. Then play a game using loud and soft voices, asking your child to tell you which voice you used.

Cleaning up: Make clean-up a part of your everyday play experience. Before going on to the next activity, pick up the toys or wash off the table. When you are doing this, talk about how you want the space to be clean for the next person who needs to use it.

Helping others: Kids learn by watching. Whenever an opportunity arises to help someone, take it. If you see an elderly woman struggling with a grocery cart, ask if you can help. If you see a child who looks lost or one who needs a push on the swing, offer to help.

Caring for pets: Whenever your child pets, holds, or plays with an animal, make sure he does it with kindness and thinks about how the animal might feel.

20

Potty Training Tips for Boys

Age Range: 24 months and up

Boys are notoriously slower to train than girls, although subsequent children tend to be faster than firsts, so be patient.

* Go shopping for "big-kid" underpants and splurge a little on whatever ones he wants.
* Provide non-nagging reminders: "I have to go again. Do you?"
* If you are buying a child-sized potty, skip (or remove) the urine guard—it doesn't really keep things clean, and it may get in the way or even bump or scratch him.
* Personalize the potty with stickers or paints.
* Teach him to use the potty sitting first—this makes things easier since both urination and bowel movements go into the toilet and often come together.
* Look for signs that he has to go, which include hopping, clutching himself, and "the look."
* Have him watch Daddy and older brothers to learn how to urinate standing up (once he is toilet-trained). Use toilet-training targets to encourage good aim: float O-cereals, store-bought targets, or put a non-slip bathtub sticker on the toilet bowl.
* Put a drop of blue food coloring in the toilet water…he'll be delighted to turn it green when he urinates.
* Praise and reward success: whoop it up or call Grandma to share the big news. Don't make a big deal of accidents, but make sure the child is in on the clean-up process.

21

Potty Training Tips for Girls

Age Range: 24 months and up

- Go shopping for "big-kid" underpants and splurge a little on whatever ones she wants.
- Provide non-nagging reminders: "I have to go again. Do you?"
- Let her choose and decorate the potty.
- Some girls want to stand after seeing fathers and older brothers do it. Let her try and see it's messy when you're not properly equipped—she'll sit back down.
- Be sure she watches women so she can imitate. Try modeling with a doll or stuffed animal on a potty while she's on hers.
- Wipe from the front to back, especially when she has a bowel movement.
- Look for signs that she has to go, such as squeezing her legs together or acting antsy.
- Put a drop of blue food coloring in the toilet water…she'll be delighted to turn it green when she urinates.
- Praise and reward success: whoop it up or call Grandma to share the big news. Don't make a big deal of accidents, but make sure the child is in on the clean-up process.

Words of Wisdom: *When I was potty training the kids, I kept a potty in the back of the van. That way we always had something in case of emergencies, and it worked out when they were afraid to go at the mall.*

—Jack, Ramona, California

22

Phone Fun

Age Range: 24 months and up

The phone will ring at least once a day. Your toddler may be fascinated with the way voices come out of nowhere, or she may be scared. In order to help her understand that she is talking to real people she knows and loves, try the following:

- Take pictures of the family members your child might talk to on the phone. Keep them in a box next to the phone. When someone calls, pull out the picture so the child knows to whom he or she is talking.
- If your child likes to hear the voice coming through the phone but doesn't say a word, try giving her a puppet and encourage her to let the puppet talk to the voice on the phone.

23

TV- and Computer-Time Tips

Age Range: 30 months and up

The American Academy of Pediatrics recommends no more than one to two hours of age-appropriate, educational programming per day, and no TV for children under two. Many parents lump any screen time into that, so include the time your children play on the computer. The TV has been a dependable child-sitter for many, so how can you wean yourself and your child?

* Give your child daily tickets that she can turn in to you if she wants to watch a show. Each ticket is worth thirty minutes—you determine how many tickets she gets.
* Tape a piece of your child's artwork over the TV when it's not in use. That way you won't be tempted to turn it on without thinking.
* Sit down and watch TV with your child so that you can talk about what is going on or use words or phrases from the show later on.
* There's a lot of educational and interactive software available. Some libraries offer the programs available for check out. Most have bright colors and goofy sounds. Sit with your child and use the computer as you would a game.

24

Naptime Tricks

Age Range: 30 months and up

* Wear your child out as naptime draws near. A chasing game or tickle fest may be just the trick! Then slow the child down with a quiet, predictable, restful ritual—a song reserved just for naptime or a brief tummy massage.
* Don't let her think she'll be missing anything fun while she's sleeping. Tell her you'll be paying bills, making phone calls, or accomplishing some other activity that she knows keeps you from playing with her.
* Have your child put a favorite doll or stuffed animal down for a nap at the same time. Pretend the toy really doesn't want to take a nap, and ask her to help her playpal unwind. As she soothes her friend to sleep, she'll be lulled to dreamland as well.
* Create a special nap space that she can associate with happy slumber—a sleeping bag, a play tent or playhouse, or a favorite blanket and pillow by a sunny window.

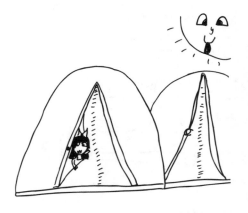

25

Exercise Fun

Age Range: 30 months and up

Physical play helps your toddler learn how her body works and allows her to become more coordinated. It stimulates her appetite for healthy meals and helps her to nap regularly and sleep better at night.

Build physical activity into your daily routine: Toddlers are notoriously energetic, so use this to your advantage by scheduling active play for opportune times—like before a typically grouchy period.

Make exercise fun: Twirl and dance to music, tumble all the way down the hall, or pretend to be a favorite thing (a growing flower stretching all the way to the sun or a race car charging through the finish line).

Get physical: You're probably his favorite playmate, so you'll be his best motivator...and it might even help moms shed any lingering baby fat!

Take it outside: The sun and the wind make for great play buddies who are sure to wear your toddler out!

26

Early Learning Games

Reading Tips

Age Range: 15 months and up

* Pick books with clear, easy words that go along with the pictures.
* Name the objects in the pictures as you go.
* Don't feel like you have to read the story word for word. Pick a few key words and make up your own story that goes along with the pictures.
* Find books with funny words, rhymes, and pictures.
* Find ways to bring the book you're reading to life. Find a book written about a picnic, the zoo, visiting grandma, baking a cake, whale-watching, a farm or candy factory, and then take a field trip to do the activity or visit the location in person.
* Make reading a regular part of your daily routine or bedtime ritual.

27

Blowing Know How

Age Range: 15 to 18 months

Materials
Large straws
Ping-pong ball, feather, Cheerios

The cause and effect action of blowing through a straw to make an object move will delight your toddler. Blowing games can be played on uncarpeted floors, tabletops, or inside the lid to a clothes box. To begin, hold the straw up to your own mouth, and show your child how to blow through the straw. Let him feel the air that comes out of the end. Then put the straw up to his mouth and put his hand at the end of the straw to feel for the air. Put a ping-pong ball down on a smooth surface and begin blowing. At first, blow alongside your child so he can see the process. Try blowing other small, light objects like a feather or piece of cereal. Make up racing games by drawing a line on the surface for the starting point and then a line a few feet away to mark the finish point.

28

Hard and Soft

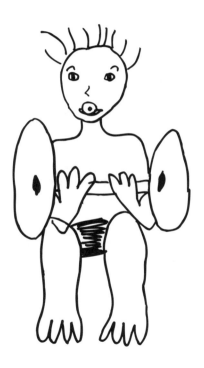

Age Range: 18 to 21 months

Go around the house collecting hard and soft objects. Put them into a container. Show each object to your child, allowing her to touch it, and use the word hard or soft to describe it. Then let the toddler take one item out of the container at a time and encourage her to say whether it is hard or soft. Once she's gotten the hang of it, put one item at a time into a big bag, let her reach in, feel the item, and then tell you if it is hard or soft. Ask her to guess what the item is without looking into the bag.

· ·

Words of Wisdom: *Puzzles have always been a nightmare to keep together in our house until I devised a plan. I mark a number on the puzzle and then put the same number on the back of all the pieces. The small puzzle pieces go into a Ziploc bag with the same number on it.*

—Becky, Batavia, Illinois

29

Writing Practice

Age Range: 18 to 21 months

Materials
Large rectangular cake pan or cookie tray
Sand, sugar, or flour

Fill the cake pan or tray with sand, sugar, or flour. Show your child how to draw lines or pictures. Take a big piece of paper and make the shape of a letter. Let him practice drawing the same shape into the sand. Try doing an add-on picture where you make one line and then your child adds on the next line to make a new design. Describe the feel of the sand, sugar, or flour as rough, soft, grainy, or smooth.

30

Counting Songs

Age Range: 18 to 21 months

Toddlers learn how to count by hearing numbers over and over. Hearing them in song form makes the learning even more fun. There are many counting songs—"This Old Man" is a favorite.

> This old man, he played one,
> He played nick-knack on my thumb.
> With a nick-knack, paddy-whack,
> Give a dog a bone,
> This old man came rolling home.

Sing the rest of the verses making these substitutions in the first and second line, or make up some of your own.

> Two on my shoe
> Three on my knee
> Four on my door
> Five on a hive
> Six on some sticks
> Seven all the way to Heaven
> Eight on my gate
> Nine on my spine
> Ten once again

31

Texture Mat

Age Range: 18 months and up

Materials
Contact paper
Nature items

Use a large piece of contact paper, preferably no smaller than 2'x 2'. Place the contact paper so that the sticky side is facing up. Place your collected nature materials onto the sticky side, making sure to leave four inches on each edge clear of material. Then turn the entire piece of contact paper over and stick it straight onto your tile, wood, or linoleum flooring. (The contact paper is easy to pull up later, so it won't leave a mess.) In the meantime, the kids will have a great time walking all over the different textures, touching them with their hands, and watching them change shape. It's also fun to masking tape a piece of contact paper to the floor sticky-side-up so the kids can feel "stuck in the mud!"

32

Silly Book

Age Range: 21 to 24 months

Materials
Notebook
Magazines (wildlife or children's magazines work well)

Go through magazines and cut out large pictures of people, animals, or cartoon characters that have heads, bodies, and legs. Glue each picture onto one right hand page of the notebook. Once you have at least ten pictures glued in the notebook, cut the pages equally into thirds so that when you flip a page the head or face will switch to be sitting on a different body. The bodies and legs should also be interchangeable so that the animals, people, or cartoon characters will look mismatched and odd when put together. This book can also be created using faces only. Make sure that the faces you choose cover most of the piece of paper.

33

Texture Box

Age Range: 21 to 24 months

Materials
Shallow tie box
Pieces of textured fabric or paper

Feeling various textures and then learning the words that describe them allows a toddler to have a better understanding of the world around her as well as learn new words to describe the things she feels. Cut a hole in the top of the box big enough so that your child's fingers can fit through. Place a piece of textured fabric—sand paper, velvet, cotton, or burlap—into the box. Let her feel it for a few minutes and then you feel it. Describe the sensations you feel. Encourage your child to touch it again as you describe what she is feeling. Use one-word descriptions so that she can begin to recognize the words that describe various textures.

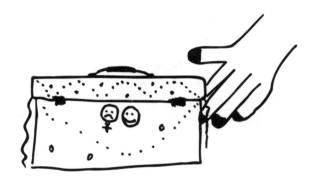

34

Word Play

Age Range: 24 to 30 months

When your child starts speaking, take his first words and build on them to make real sentences. If he says, "Want milk," you might say, "I want milk for breakfast." Try using favorite words in silly combinations, such as "Willie wanted milk for kitty, bitsy, mite, and smee." Or try to incorporate the words into a familiar song melody, replacing the words to a song like "Twinkle, Twinkle Little Star."

....

Words of Wisdom: *I do a lot of baby-sitting. But for two-year-olds and up, I make a point of calling myself a "kid-sitter," and I'm always sure to "scold" parents when they casually throw around the B-word in front of the children. The kids always crack up, and it makes them feel more mature.*

—Penny, Sayre, Pennsylvania

35

Recording Fun

Age Range: 24 to 30 months

Kids love to hear their own voices. They like to listen to recordings of the family eating dinner, traveling in the car, playing a game, or any familiar sounds. Buy tapes with recording lengths of three, five, or ten minutes. That way you won't have to be continually trying to find the recording you're looking for. Sing songs, read stories, make messages for friends, and tape-record your phone conversations to play before naptime. Growth of a child's vocabulary is directly related to the words and conversations he hears, so talk it up, and when you aren't around to talk, play a tape of your voice.

36

My Picture Flash Cards

Age Range: 30 to 36 months

Take clear and simple photos of family members, the child's room and belongings, the backyard, play equipment, pets, and friends. Use them as flash cards. Point to the item in the picture and tell your child what it is, who it is, or what the child does with it. Once he can name what is in each picture, take another set of pictures to include action shots, such as feeding the dog, eating breakfast, playing in the sand, or kissing mom. Show him the cards again, but this time add the action words to the description using a total of three words or less per card. Make it fun by clapping with each response, saying the words with him, or making up a funny story about the picture once he says the correct word.

37

Color Search

Materials
White paper
Colored construction paper
Crayons
Paper bag

Take a crayon and draw a blotch of color on the white paper, or pick out a colored piece of construction paper. Tell your child what color you'll be searching for, then go exploring around the house for things that are that same color. Put whatever found items that match the color you're hunting for inside the paper bag. If they won't fit in the bag, simply point them out. When finished, sit down and pull each item out of the bag one at a time, and talk about the color again. Once your child begins to recognize the colors, fill the paper bag with an assortment of colored items, set the colored pieces of construction paper on the ground, and have her put the items on top of the construction paper according to color.

38

Shape Dance

Age Range: 30 to 36 months

Materials
Sidewalk chalk

Take the sidewalk chalk and draw several different shapes on a hard surface. Then ask your child to do some sort of motor movement inside of the shape: stand on one foot, dance, hop, wiggle, or sit. If space permits, draw a small and large size of the same shape so your child also has to think about the size of the shape he chooses.

••

Words of Wisdom: *I used to hate throwing away my daughter's character shampoo bottles when they had such adorable tops. So we started gluing them to the top of a wooden dowel. Now she has a whole set of homemade puppets.*
—Kristen, San Antonio, Texas

39

Letter Book

Age Range: 30 to 36 months

Materials
Large sheets of white construction paper
Magazines
Scissors
Glue

This book is fun to make over a long period of time. Decoratively write one letter of the alphabet in the top right- or left-hand corner of the construction paper. Look through the magazines for pictures of people, places, or things that begin with that letter. Cut them out and glue them onto the page. Set the finished page aside until you've completed enough letter pages to make a book.

40

Food-Time Fun

Kitchen Helpers

Age Range: 15 months and up

Toddlers love to do exactly what you are doing. If you're making dinner they are going to be right at your side, so why not give them something to do. Teach them how to wash their hands before working with food. Buy a small stepstool so they can stand next to you at counter level then give them one or more of the following jobs:

* Ripping lettuce
* Spinning the salad
* Rolling out dough
* Wiping off the table
* Dumping ingredients into a bowl
* Shaking homemade salad dressing
* Stirring, mixing, or spreading
* Washing vegetables
* Sweeping up whatever falls on the floor
* Setting napkins out on the table
* Putting silverware on the table

41

Tea-Party Dough

Age Range: 15 months and up

Materials
Mixing bowl
1 cup peanut butter
1 cup corn syrup
1½ cups powdered sugar
1½ cups powdered milk

You can eat this dough. Really!
Mix ingredients together in the bowl. Additional powdered milk may be needed to make the dough not-so sticky. Knead. Use cookie cutters or design your own shapes. If the tea party idea doesn't fly, try having a birthday party. Birthday candles are fun to stick in the dough.

....

Words of Wisdom: *My daughter loves to cut sliced cheese into shapes with cookie cutters and put it on top of casseroles. Place the cheese when the casserole is about five minutes from being done and return it to the oven for about five minutes until it is just melted.*

—JoEllen, Raleigh, North Carolina

42

Creative Mealtimes

Age Range: 15 months and up

Eating at the table every day gets boring, especially during the winter months when rain or snow might keep you indoors more than you'd like. Why not try an indoor picnic? Set a blanket on the floor, make a lunch, and pack a picnic basket. Play games on the blanket. Or create a day at the beach. Turn the heat up in your house so everyone can wear bathing suits or shorts, blow up a beach ball, and play catch. Grill hot dogs and hamburgers on a minigrill set up on the kitchen counter. Eating the same kind of food each day in exactly the same order can get boring, too! Try reversing the order of your meals—eat dinner foods for breakfast and breakfast foods for dinner—or create a meal where every food is the same color. Make a rule that one night a week everybody has to sing conversations instead of simply talking.

43

Pudding Paint

Age Range: 15 months and up

Materials
Instant pudding
Food coloring

This painting can be done on a high-chair tray, on finger-painting paper, on a cookie sheet, or in a clean bathtub. Mix up the pudding according to package instructions. Put the pudding into plastic containers according to how many colors you'd like to have. Add the food coloring. Once the pudding is mixed, set the containers in front of your child. Encourage him to use the pudding as one would use finger paint. If your child is in the bathtub, let him paint his body with the pudding, but make sure to keep him sitting down so he doesn't slip. Your child will enjoy the texture of the pudding squishing through his fingers as well as the yummy taste.

44

Rice Fun

Age Range: 18 to 21 months

Make the largest batch of rice that will fit in your saucepan. Let it cool. Put a plastic tablecloth on the floor. Dump the rice out on the tablecloth making a hill. Use spoons, cups, rolling pins, or other kitchen utensils to mold and play with the rice. Spoon the rice into cupcake tins, use cookie cutters to make rice cakes, squish the rice into balls and roll them up and down the tablecloth. When finished, throw the rice away and wash the tablecloth.

Words of Wisdom: *My kids used to complain about stale sandwiches at lunch until I started making their sandwiches on frozen pieces of bread. They defrost by lunchtime and are not soggy.*

—Charlie, Tifton, Georgia

45

Sorting Pasta

Age Range: 21 to 24 months

Materials
Pasta in a variety of shapes and colors
Large bowl or plastic container

Put a mixed variety of dry pasta together in the plastic container. Show your child how to sort the pasta into like piles. Place all the straight pasta in one pile and the curly in another. Or, if the pasta comes in different colors, you might sort it by color. Put all the pasta that is exactly the same in one pile. Use words to describe the different piles you are making: curly, straight, ridged, corkscrew, wide, thin, short, or long.

Words of Wisdom: *If you have toddlers who don't like to get their fingers sticky eating an apple, try using plastic corn holders.*
—Janet, Sacramento, California

46

Homemade Butter

Age Range: 24 months and up

Materials
Whipping cream
Empty baby food jar or small clear plastic container
Crackers

Pour four tablespoons of cream into the baby food jar or plastic container. Screw on the lid and shake vigorously. After a few minutes a lump of solid butter will form inside the jar. Remove the butterball and let your child spread it on crackers.

Words of Wisdom: *To prevent messes at the table, my husband bought a Rubbermaid dish drainer. We put my daughter's plate, bowl, cup—whatever—on there, and messes stay confined to the drainer instead of all over the table. Then you just pick the whole thing up when it comes time to wash everything.*
—Jane, Novato, California

47

Homemade Ice Cream

Age Range: 24 months and up

Materials
5 cups crushed ice
3 tablespoons salt
½ cup whole milk
½ teaspoon vanilla extract

1 gallon-sized sealable plastic bag
1 quart-sized sealable plastic bag
1 tablespoon sugar

Put the ice into the large plastic bag and sprinkle with the salt. Pour the milk, sugar, and vanilla into the small plastic bag. Seal it well, removing as much air as possible. Place the small bag into the large ice-filled bag, making sure it is completely surrounded by ice. Seal the large bag and shake vigorously, or go outside and play catch with the bag, making sure to throw it only a few feet. After about five minutes, take the small bag from the ice, open the bag to add any additional ingredients, then knead the bag to mix it together. Spoon into a bowl and eat!

Flavor Ideas: Chocolate (add one tablespoon chocolate syrup); Chocolate chip (add chopped chocolate chips); Strawberry (add two tablespoons mashed fresh strawberries or one tablespoon strawberry jam); Cookies and Cream (add crushed cookies)

48

Playing the Food Manners Game

Age Range: 24 months and up

Toddlers learn manners entirely by example, so be a good role model. Use your dramatic skills to attract your child's attention when you do things like put your napkin on your lap, wipe your mouth, or wait to speak until you've chewed your food. Work on one manner at a time for many weeks until your toddler performs the desired behavior without being reminded. Make a game out of it. Let your child be the mommy or daddy and correct your manners. Let him guess what you are doing wrong. Or, throw a pretend birthday or tea party so you can practice saying "please," using your spoon to stir your tea, or asking for food to be passed. Remind your child before the meal begins what manner you are working on that day.

Expectations: Twenty-four months and up: children can stop dropping food deliberately on the floor. Thirty-six months and up: children can say "please," "thank you," and "excuse me." They should not talk with food in their mouths and can use napkins, spoons, and forks correctly. They should be able to sit at the table without distracting or disturbing others for up to fifteen minutes.

49

Egg in a Bun

Materials
4 hamburger buns
Soft butter or margarine
4 eggs
Salt and pepper
4 slices of cheese
Round cookie cutter

Preheat the oven to 350ºF (180ºC). Place all of the ingredients on a table. Using the cookie cutter, cut a round hole in the top half of the buns, and remove the cut bun circles with a fork. Butter the insides of the buns and place them on a baking sheet. Break an egg into each hole and lightly sprinkle with salt and pepper. Bake in the oven for twenty minutes, then place the cheese slice over the bun. Bake five more minutes or until the cheese is melted. Serve warm.

••

Words of Wisdom: *If an egg ever cracks on the floor, use a basting syringe to suck it up; it's much easier than using a cloth.*
—Alice, Newport Beach, California

Baked Bread Sandwiches

Materials

Frozen loaf of white or wheat bread
 (the kind that has to rise)
Garlic salt
1/3 lb. ham, thinly sliced
1/3 lb. provolone cheese, thinly sliced
1/3 lb. hard salami, thinly sliced
1/3 lb. Swiss cheese, thinly sliced
2 egg yolks, beaten
Flour
Yields 8 to 12 servings

Thaw the bread and let it rise, covered, in a warm spot for one hour. Punch down and knead with a small amount of flour. On a floured surface, roll the dough out into a twelve-by-sixteen inch rectangle. Sprinkle with garlic salt. Tear the meat into bite-sized pieces and layer it over the bread. Tear the cheeses into bite-sized pieces and layer them over the meat. Layering and rolling are good jobs for little hands. Start at the long end and roll up tightly in jelly-roll fashion. Pinch the ends together tightly and curve the roll to form a crescent. Brush with the beaten egg yolk. Place it on cookie sheet and let it rest twenty minutes. Bake at 375°F (190°C) for twenty-five to thirty minutes or until golden brown. Let it rest for a few minutes before thinly slicing. If you are taking this on a picnic, wait until you get there to slice it!

Words of Wisdom: *A ball of extra dough, some flour, and a plastic knife go a long way!*
—Anna, Chicago, Illinois

51

Honey Lover's Chicken

Materials

4 whole boneless chicken breasts
2 tablespoons flour
$\frac{1}{2}$ cup corn-flake crumbs
1 teaspoon salt

$\frac{1}{2}$ cup melted butter or margarine
2 tablespoons prepared mustard
$\frac{1}{2}$ cup yellow cornmeal
$\frac{1}{4}$ teaspoon paprika

Preheat the oven to 350°F (180°C). Remove the skin from the chicken breast. Cut each boneless breast in half lengthwise. Blend the flour and the mustard into the melted butter until smooth. Dip the chicken pieces in the butter mixture and coat well with crumbs and seasonings. Place on a shallow, foil-lined pan and drip the remaining butter mixture on top. Bake for thirty minutes or until tender. Dip it into honey or any other dip your child likes, and eat. This can also be refrigerated and taken for lunch.

Words of Wisdom: *Don't make special meals. Tell the child to take one bite to "try" the food, then if he doesn't like it, he doesn't have to eat it (the child won't starve!). Eventually, he'll learn to like foods he didn't like at first.*
—Laura, Golden Valley, Minnesota

52

Yummy Parfaits

Materials
4 cups fresh fruit
1 cup whipped topping
2 small boxes instant pudding
Garnishes: raisins, coconut, nuts, carob chips, etc.
Yields 6 to 8 servings

Get out clear glasses of any kind (dessert, wine, or water). Make the pudding according to box directions. Prepare the fruit by washing and cutting it into small pieces. Put the garnishes in separate containers or readily available piles. Begin layering the pudding, fruit, and garnishes in any way you like. Be creative! Top with whipped topping.

Words of Wisdom: *My son will only eat pears if I make them look like a mouse; place half a pear cut-side down on the plate, then add raisin eyes and nose, slivered almonds or carrot peels for the ears, and a string-cheese tail.*

—Patrice, Henderson, Texas

53

Ice-Cream-Cone Cakes

Materials
Flat bottomed ice-cream cones
Cake mix
Frosting mix
Cake decorations
Muffin pan
Yields 12 to 15

Prepare the cake mix according to directions. Spoon the batter into the cones until they are ⅔ full. Place the cones in the muffin pan and bake at 350ºF (180ºC) for twelve to fifteen minutes. When cool, frost and decorate.

··

Words of Wisdom: *There are all kinds of ways to make exciting ice cubes for parties. Fill ice cube trays with one or two berries, cover with warm water, and freeze overnight. Or add food coloring or freeze fruit juice for ice cubes of a solid color.*

—Nancy, Shorewood, Minnesota

54

Butterfly Sandwiches

Cutting food into fun shapes is a good way to get children interested in eating. The butterfly sandwich is one that has been cut diagonally, then halves are reversed to look like a butterfly. Serve this sandwich open-faced, spread with peanut butter, cream cheese, or butter, then decorate the butterfly with colorful fruit, vegetables, raisins, banana slices, grated cheese, meat slices, or anything your child likes to eat. Let her do the decorating. Add two thin slices of celery for the antennae.

Words of Wisdom: *Last summer I discovered a perfect Popsicle drip catcher. I took a few plastic drink-container lids from a fast food restaurant and stuck the Popsicle stick through them.*
—Beth, Minneapolis, Minnesota

55

Designer Pancakes

Materials

1½ cups milk	4 tablespoons vegetable oil
2 eggs	2 teaspoons baking powder
1½ cups flour	Oil or butter for frying

Put the ingredients in a bowl and mix. Heat a skillet over medium heat, and add two tablespoons of oil. When a drop of water dances on the surface of the skillet, you are ready to begin your art! Using a large spoon, dribble the pancake mix into the skillet, making a design. Make your designs small enough to fit inside a pancake. Cook the design for thirty seconds. Pour one-fourth cup of the remaining batter on top of the design and wait until the pancake has bubbles on it before turning it over (one to two minutes). Turn the pancake and brown other side. Cover with syrup or jam and eat! Kids may also like to make pancake people with fat arms and legs, and raisins, blueberries, or chocolate chip eyes.

....

Words of Wisdom: *To keep my daughter from eating too many snacks between meals, I made some snack coupons. I gave her four a day. Three were to use during the day between meals and the last before bed.*

—Amanda, Omaha, Nebraska

56

Bath and Water Play

Playing the Water Game

Age Range: 15 months and up

Water safety is a major concern for parents of toddlers. A toddler's curious nature and lack of fear might lead him to walk directly into a creek or reach for a toy floating in a pool without thinking about the consequences of falling in. Here are some tips to keep your child safe:

* **Never leave a child alone around water**. It is possible to drown in a few inches. Don't be fooled into thinking blow up flotation devices will keep your child safe. Assign one parent to lifeguard duty at all times.
* Before taking kids near water, make sure one supervising adult knows how to swim.
* Learn CPR.
* If you have children of different ages, bring a blow-up pool to place away from the lake or ocean so that older kids who are ready to play in the ocean or lake have the opportunity to play while infants have their own water fun in the baby pool.
* Establish clear rules to be followed regarding water play. No turning bath water on without a parent in attendance, and no getting into the baby pool or bathtub without a parent.
* Teach kids to appreciate that water is fun but can also be dangerous.

57

Bubbles Away

Age Range: 15 months and up

Bubble Recipe
1 cup green dishwashing detergent
$\frac{1}{2}$ cup glycerine, available at drug stores
$\frac{1}{2}$ cup water

Bubble fun will keep toddlers busy for hours. There are all sorts of things around the house that can be used as bubble wands. A wooden spoon with a hole in it, a length of wire curved into whatever shape, or a pair of old glasses with the lenses removed. There are also a variety of bubble wands of all shapes and sizes available in stores. Blow a bubble high in the air and try to catch it with your hands or with one of the bubble wands. Let bubbles float to the ground then try to stomp on them. Count how many bubbles you can blow before one doesn't turn out. Use a bubble wand that blows consecutive bubbles. Run with it as you blow and watch the bubble stream left in your wake.

58

Rock Waves

Age Range: 15 to 18 months

Toddlers are fascinated by cause-and-effect reactions. Collect a small pile of rocks of various sizes. Make sure to check the rocks for choking hazard and take the small ones out of the pile. Fill a tub or bucket with water. Let your child drop one rock at a time into the tub and watch what kind of splash it creates. Lift the rock high in the air and then drop it. Take that same rock and hold it just inches from the water before letting it go. Try dropping a really big rock and see what kind of splash it makes. Once the rocks are in the tub, point out all the different colors that show up when the rocks are wet and shiny.

Words of Wisdom: *Whenever I was out in the yard gardening, I'd give my son his own sprinkler. Take a plastic milk bottle and poke holes in the bottom with a hammer. Fill it with water and let your child water plants.*
—Jill, Fort Drum, New York

59

Fun with Ice

Age Range: 18 to 21 months

Ice in all forms interests toddlers: the way it melts, how an object gets stuck inside of it, or the way it slides all over the place, sometimes eluding a toddler's hands.

* Add food coloring to a cup of water. Pour the colored water into ice cube trays. Make many different-colored ice cubes. Once frozen, put two different-colored cubes into a plastic bag and watch them melt. Notice what color the two different-colored ice cubes create when mixed together.
* Cut an old paper milk carton in half. Fill it with water and put some plastic toys inside of it. Freeze. Put the frozen block into the bathtub and watch it melt until the frozen toy emerges. (Be sure the toy passes the choke test.)
* Make a block of ice in a milk carton as above. Gather coins, rocks, silverware, or other objects that warm up in the sun and place them outside until warm. Set the warm objects on the block of ice until the ice melts, leaving an indentation of the object.

Tub Time Games

Age Range: 18 months and up

Bath time ballads: Turn on a radio to a fun station or play a cassette your child likes and sing into the shampoo bottle. If you have a hard time getting your child out of the bath, try using the length of a song as the time limit.

Kitchen arsenal: Go through the kitchen and gather funnels, a turkey baster, squeeze bottles, wire whisks, measuring cups, colanders, and any other plastic supplies that could be used in the bath. Hold the colander up and pour water through it to create rain, use the turkey baster to take water from the tub and squeeze it into various cups, or use a wire wisk to stir up the fading bath bubbles.

Tub bubbles: Go to the hardware store and buy a few different sizes of soft plastic tubing. Use it to blow bubbles into the bath. Make sure one piece of tubing is long enough so you can sit outside the bath with the tube under the water and surprise your child with blasts of bubbles rising to the surface.

Words of Wisdom: *In my son's bathroom, we hung a pulley over the bathtub that holds a basket of bath toys. When bath time is over, we simply hoist it up and out of the way and let the toys drip dry.*
—Sally, Belleville, Michigan

61

Water Band

Age Range: 18 to 21 months

A stream of water hitting large objects makes a lovely and varied sound. Collect old pots, buckets, garbage-can lids, recycling bins, cookie trays, and anything else you can find that might make a cool sound. Lean the items up against a fence, house, wall, or garage door. Attach a spray nozzle to the hose. Spray each item high, low, hard, and soft to see what kind of sounds you can make. Compose a melody as you adjust the spray to vary the sound.

Words of Wisdom: *I bought a gardener's pad to put on the floor next to the bath. Now I can kneel on the floor for as long as my baby wants to splash and gurgle.*

—Linda, Overland Park, Kansas

62

Wading Pool Basketball

Age Range: 18 to 21 months

Fill a child's wading pool with a few inches of water. Put all sizes of floating balls into the pool. Tape a plastic colander to the side of the pool, or set a laundry basket on the grass next to the pool. Show your child how to throw the balls into the basket. Collect all the balls, put them in the laundry basket, and step outside of the pool turning the wading pool into one big basket. See how far away you can stand from the pool and still make your shots.

• •

Words of Wisdom: *When visiting the beach, bring an inflatable baby pool and fill it with buckets of ocean water. Keep it next to your beach chair so your toddler can play in it when you need to take breaks from supervising ocean play.*

63

Rainbow Surprise

Age Range: 21 to 24 months

When the sun shines after a rain shower, our eyes are sometimes treated to a beautiful rainbow. Seven colors appear in every rainbow: red, orange, yellow, green, blue, indigo, and violet. Most of the time only four or five colors can be seen clearly. An enjoyable wet activity to do on a sunny day is to create your own rainbow. If the weather is very warm, bathing suits are a must. Turn on the garden hose, adjust the nozzle to the fine spray setting, then arch the water high into the air. Watch as the rays of the sun hit the water and create a rainbow. Talk about the different colors you see as you experiment moving the hose around. This can also be done with a sprinkler if it is put in the right spot. Find a rainbow story from the library and share it with your toddler. If a hose is not available, try using a plastic squeeze bottle filled with water.

64

Rain Games

Age Range: 21 to 24 months

Too often when the rain begins to fall children are ushered indoors. Playing outside in the rain can be the highlight of a spring or summer day. So the next time it rains, put on your raincoats, boots, or bathing suits and splash in the puddles, make mud pies, and squish wet grass between your toes. Set containers around the outside of your house to measure the rain, make up a tribal rain dance, or move to the beat of the rain as it falls softly or pounds the ground. Don't forget to look straight up to the sky and watch it as it falls on your face, then open your mouth to taste the drops.

65

Sponge Tag

Age Range: 24 to 30 months

Materials
Buckets and Sponges

Nothing thrills a toddler quite as much as participating in a get Mommy or Daddy game. Fill two buckets with warm water. Put three or four sponges in each bucket. To begin the game, stand about ten feet apart with each person standing next to his or her own bucket, or if more than two people are playing, divide up into equal teams and have each team stand next to a bucket. Say, "Ready, set, go!" and start throwing the sponges at each other. Once your child gets the hang of the game, you can play tag with the sponges. The person who is "it" gets the sponges soaked and ready for throwing, and everyone else runs. When someone is hit by a sponge, they become the next "it." Toddlers also like to try to hit a sitting target, so if you're game, sit on the ground and let your child throw the sponges at you.

Words of Wisdom: *My son loves to take an outdoor foot bath. I fill a wash pan with soapy water, ask him to take off his shoes and socks, then massage his foot while I name all the parts of his foot.*

—John, Peru, Indiana

66

Squirt Away

Age Range: 24 to 30 months

Materials
Plastic soda bottles
Water squirt gun
Ping-pong balls

Fill the plastic soda bottles with water or sand so they won't fall over when squirted. Place the ping-pong balls on top of the water bottles. Stand back two feet and try to knock the ping-pong balls off the bottles by shooting the squirt gun. Or have a contest to see who can knock the balls off first. Divide the bottles in half, so each person gets the same amount of balls to aim at, then squirt away until all the balls are knocked off. Another fun contest is to work together against the clock. Set the timer for one minute and see how many balls the two of you can squirt off.

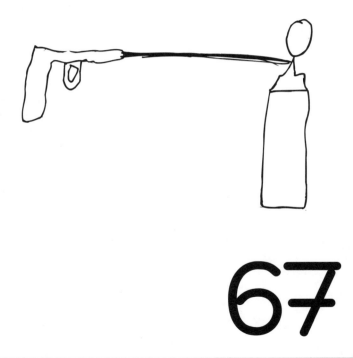

67

Wiggle Slide

Age Range: 30 to 36 months

Materials
Plastic sheet at least 12 feet long (can use cut plastic garbage bag)
Hose with a sprinkler
Grass to put plastic sheet on

Put the plastic sheet outside on the grass and turn on the hose or sprinkler. Get your bathing suit on and join your child for a wet, wiggling experience. Younger children might crawl as they enjoy this slippery experience. Lie on your backs and squirm, or move your arms up and down like you are making a snow angel. Older toddlers will run and slide on the plastic. On a hot day, nothing beats sprinkler fun.

··

Words of Wisdom: *When my two-year-old started slamming doors, I would jump out of my chair in fright. Another mother suggested I put towels over the top of the door. Now I don't worry about little fingers…or noise.*
—Liza, Chesterland, Ohio

68

Bottled Fun

Age Range: 30 to 36 months

Toddlers are often mesmerized with the many things water can do. Give them their first taste of science with these two bottle experiments.

Ocean waves: Fill a clean sixteen-ounce plastic soda bottle one-third full with water. Add a few drops of food coloring, glitter, or beads. Fill the rest of the bottle with baby oil. Glue the cap securely onto the bottle. Gently rock the bottle to create ocean waves. Shake it up when you are done, then watch as the water and oil separate as the mixture settles.

Tornado in a bottle: Use two large, clear, plastic soda bottles. Fill one two-thirds full with water and add a few drops of food coloring. Invert the other bottle so that it sits on top of the first bottle with the openings together. Wind tape lightly around the necks of the bottles so that no water can leak out. The top bottle should be securely balanced on top of the bottom bottle. Hold the bottles with two hands and swirl the water around, then turn it upside down and see what happens.

Bedtime

Bedtime Safari

Age Range: 15 months and up

Once your child is all ready for bed, play this fun-in-the-dark game. Hide stuffed animals around the house or bedroom. Turn off all the lights and use a flashlight to hunt for the animals that are hiding. Even if your child helps you hide the animals, the hiding places look different and more exciting in the dark. Hold hands as you go from place to place, letting your child hold the flashlight as you follow along.

Words of Wisdom: *Encourage quiet mornings by filling a basket in your child's room with books, crayons, puzzles, or other quiet games each bedtime. This independent play allows you a few hours of sleep.*

—Carrie Jo, Raleigh, North Carolina

70

Sleep Mobile

Age Range: 15 months and up

Materials
Small wooden dowels (from a craft or hardware store)
Toys, stuffed animals, ornaments
String

Make a peaceful mobile with favorite toys or stuffed animals to lull your child to sleep. Cut the wooden dowels to various lengths. Tie the string to the end of each dowel and then attach a toy, wooden airplane, small stuffed animal, or ornament to the end of the string. Attach each of these individual dowels to a center string that will hang from the ceiling. Make a small notch in the center or balance point of each dowel so the string won't slide. Tie the first dowel to the center string, followed by the next dowel five to eight inches below. Your child will enjoy looking up to see her favorite toys as she falls asleep.

71

Bedtime Chart

Age Range: 18 months and up

Going to sleep and leaving the excitement and action of family life is not always easy for children. It helps if they can see all the steps that actually lead up to going to bed. Make a chart with drawn pictures of what your child does each night that lead up to bedtime. You may even want to take real pictures and put them up on the chart. It's fun for him to go up to the pictures and know what to do next without being told. This is especially evident around two years old, when he wants to be more independent. Make sure to give lots of smiles and hugs as each step is completed.

••

Words of Wisdom: *We make up songs all the time at our house. One of James's favorites when he was just getting used to his big-boy bed was this: "Close the door, turn off the lights, turn on the music, and say night-night." It made lying down for naps much easier. We later added the verse, "Let's read a story, just Mommy and me. James loves Mommy and Mommy loves me."*

—Leigh Ann, Jacksonville, Florida

72

Flashlight Fun

Age Range: 18 months and up

- Take turns moving the light beam all around the room while the other person chases it—leaping around, crouching down low, rolling on the floor, and so forth.
- Arm both yourself and your child with flashlights and play dueling flashlights—chase the other's beams with your own. Take turns being the leader.
- Tape dark cut-outs of simple shapes over the lens of the flashlight. Watch how the shape is distorted by moving the flashlight around the room.

. . . .

Words of Wisdom: *We keep my son's bedtime rituals like reading, rubbing his back, and singing confined to his bed. If he gets up in the night, we repeat some of the rituals only after he's back in his own bed.*
—Dean, Billings, Montana

73

Dream Time

Age Range: 18 months and up

When kids are scared to go to sleep or complain of bad dreams, it helps to make up a dream together. Before your child falls asleep, make up the dream that she wants to have that night. Get her involved in all the details, making sure she has a guardian or helper in the story. Send her off to sleep with the positive thought that she will dream her own dream instead of a scary one.

Words of Wisdom: *We installed a dimmer switch when we decorated our daughter's nursery. We get her in her pajamas and read a story when it's bright, lower it for songs, and take it down to nearly nothing as she dozes off.*

—Jade, Evergreen, Colorado

74

I Am Thankful

Age Range: 24 months and up

The best way to go to bed is with a happy heart. Encourage your little one to spend a moment before bed talking about what she is thankful for each day. You'll be amazed—and probably quite flattered—by her appreciation of some little thing you did. Watch her light up when you return the favor. It's a great reminder for both of you about what really matters. Take it one step further and create a jar of thanks. Write down what each of you are thankful for each night and put it in the jar. Then, on any nights she is stumped (or any time of day you are feeling like you could use a parent morale booster!), pick one and remember how good it feels to be thankful—and how easy it is to do the little things we all appreciate. Save the list or collect the scraps and periodically add them to the family scrapbook.

Words of Wisdom: *An hour before bedtime, start whispering. It will put your kids in a sleepy mood.*
—Karina, Edmond, Oklahoma

75

Monster Hunt

Age Range: 24 months and up

If your child worries about night monsters, here are a few ideas to soothe her anxiety:

* Conduct a monster hunt just before bed. With grand gestures and lots of humor, peek under the bed, in the closet, in dresser drawers, and behind the curtains and spook any monsters away!
* Make a sign for her bedroom door that reads **No Monsters Allowed in My Room**.
* Create a protection ritual—your own monster spray with a bottle of water and a little food coloring or fragrance to make it more convincing, a special hug, a certain way you tuck the blanket in—and in the morning, be sure to comment on how well it worked.
* Make a talisman—a favorite stuffed animal to stand guard, perhaps—and weave a story about how it magically turns monsters into dewdrops on the window.
* Acknowledge the fear and assure your support, but remember to use the word pretend—that all monsters, even the scariest ones, are "pretend" monsters (as are the fun ones like Elmo!).
* Keep a flashlight or light-up toy with your child.

76

Dream Catcher

Age Range: 24 months and up

A Native American legend says dream catchers filter good dreams to the sleeper and trap bad dreams in the web. To encourage nothing but sweet dreams for your little sleeper, make a simple dream catcher for his window. Purchase an embroidery hoop and take the two hoops apart. String pretty beads onto lengths of twine, yarn, or ribbon. Drape them across the smaller hoop, crisscrossing wherever you like. Continue adding the decorated string until you've created an appealing jeweled web effect. Then snap on the top. Tie a few more strings from the bottom, and embellish them with feathers and beads tied to the end. Attach a hanging loop to the top and hang this from the ceiling above his head, on the wall by his bed, or in his bedroom window.

It's Up to You

Age Range: 24 months and up

When trying to get your child to go to sleep, offer choices (all of which you can live with) to put him in charge of his nighttime rituals. Offer two kinds of children's toothpaste. Let him select his bedtime story from a few books you've chosen. Let him choose the songs, as you let him know how many songs you're willing to sing. You may even want to write down his choices and check them off so he can see the progression toward bedtime. Let him choose which toy he sleeps with, whether he gives and/or receives hugs and kisses from Mom and Dad, whether the light stays on, or whether the door is open, or cracked, or closed. With all these choices to make, he's sure to fall quickly and easily asleep!

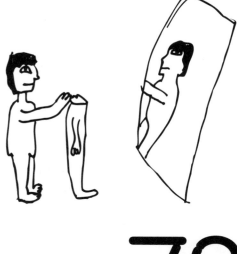

78

Feelings Today

Age Range: 30 months and up

Before bedtime, you and your child each remember a happy memory and a sad memory from the day. As kids get older, you can add other emotions: exciting, scary, angry, friendly, etc. This helps develop a ritual of keeping communication open, and it also attaches emotion to a memory and helps a child think about herself within the experience.

• •

Words of Wisdom: *Let your toddler pick out outfits for the next day the night before. We use clothespins to keep them together—this matches outfits in advance and saves time in the morning.*

—Jill, Hagerstown, Maryland

79

Story Inventions

Age Range: 30 months and up

Bedtime is the perfect time to tell made-up stories. Without pictures to look at, your child is more likely to close his eyes, relax, and interact with you. Early on, make up a character who is the child's same age and sex. The character goes to all sorts of interesting places, ones that your child shows interest in: birthday parties, school, camping, the ballet, zoo, etc. Make up a new adventure each night. Your child will look forward nightly to this time together. There is something extra special about stories made up by you!

· ·

Words of Wisdom: *We encouraged our toddler to "read" to us at night by pausing before the end of each phrase or page of his favorite storybooks and letting him fill in the blanks. He was very proud of his abilities, and we were amazed at how well he could recite his goodnight stories!*

—Ruth, Turlock, California

Pillow Pals

Age Range: 30 months and up

* Paint a personalized pillowcase with regular or glow-in-the-dark fabric paints, stencils, or rubber stamps. When you go on vacation, all you need to take is the pillowcase to feel at home in any hotel room!
* Make or buy a small purse-like pillow. Put a good-luck charm inside and hang it on the bedpost.
* Buy a pillow form and sew a simple case with a pocket big enough to fit a standard picture book (or just stitch a big pocket onto a store-bought sham). Lay it on top of your child's bed and encourage her to pick that night's bedtime story when you make the bed in the morning. Peeking out of the pillow all day, the book will give her something to look forward to.
* Use cotton, satin, or silk scraps to make soothing eye pillows. Cut out 7½ by 3½ rectangles. Turn right-side in and stitch, with a machine or by hand, along all four sides, leaving an inch hole for filling. Turn right-side out (a Popsicle stick, knitting needle, or chopstick can help), and fill it with lavender and flax seeds (at health food stores). Then stitch it up. These are great for naptime and bedtime—for parent and tot.

81

Room Decor

Canvas Growth Chart

Materials
Canvas
Fabric or acrylic paint
Wooden dowels
Ribbon

Decide how tall and wide you'd like the canvas to be, depending on your chosen design. Fold the canvas over the dowel at the top and bottom, and sew or glue with a hot glue gun. Personalize it with a name and fun art. Use stencils if you're not confident free-handing the design. Make sure to measure how far off the floor your growth chart will hang before marking off the feet and inches with a yardstick. Tie the ribbon from one side of the dowel to the other and hang your chart on the wall.

82

Colored Light

Materials
Glass jars of all sizes with lids
Food coloring

Fill the jars with water. Add a few drops of food coloring to each jar, experimenting with the amount of color. Mix the colors so all colors of the rainbow can be represented. Put the lids on the jars and arrange them on a window sill in your child's room. When the sunlight shines through the window, beautiful patterns of light can be seen.

red+yellow=orange
red+blue=purple
blue+yellow=green

• •

Words of Wisdom: *I bought large wooden knobs and painted pictures of socks, shirts, and pants on them—now my toddler's dresser drawers are coded so he can help put laundry away and get himself dressed.*

—Amanda, Wilsonville, Alabama

Learning Mat

Find or buy a carpet remnant at least four foot by four foot. Use stencils to paint on numbers, letters, or other designs. Make up a hopscotch pattern, draw a huge checker-board, or stencil big open shapes to be used as part of an obstacle course. Play musical hopscotch by turning on music while your child runs around the rug. When you stop the music and yell out a number, letter, design, or shape, the child has to run to that location and do a little dance. Make up all sorts of games to play on your learning mat.

••

Words of Wisdom: *For the child stuck on a bottom bunk, the view isn't very nice. My daughter and I decided to paint a mural on a white sheet and then staple it to the underside of her sister's top bunk.*

—Olinda, Dallas, Texas

84

Felt Garden

Why not create a garden in your child's room? Attach a large piece of felt to a piece of poster board and then attach it to the wall at floor level. You may need to attach many poster board panels if you'd like to cover the bottom half of one entire wall. Cut out different sizes and shapes of felt to be used as flower petals, stems, leaves, grass, rocks, butterflies, bugs, or birds. Let your child create the garden by arranging the felt pieces into various flower arrangements. Change your garden regularly by adding felt shapes to represent seasonal changes.

••

Words of Wisdom: *Organize your child's hair bows by taking a long one-inch-wide ribbon and attaching it to the closet pole. Clip bows to the ribbon so your child can see them all and choose.*

—Teressa, Aurora, Illinois

85

Playroom Design Tips

There are so many fun things that can be done to make a plain bedroom into an exciting, fun playroom. Here are a few tips:

- Paint one wall, a closet door, or some designed shape with blackboard paint (found at most paint stores).
- Carpet half the room and plastic-tile half the room so there is space to sit on the floor and play comfortably as well as a space for messy projects.
- Cut corkboard into the shapes of animals or trees, then attach them to the wall for a great place to hang artwork.
- Attach two large hooks to the wall so you can mount a large drawing pad. Self-adhesive Velcro pads can be stuck on the wall next to the drawing pad for the attachment of drawing materials.
- White marker board can be bought in sheets from the hardware store. Ask for white bath panel. This can be cut into shapes using a jigsaw or handsaw and then attached to the wall. Use dry-erase markers.

86

Display Treasures

There are all sorts of ways to create space to display artwork, found treasures, and projects made at home or day-care. Here are a few ideas:

❋ Install plate-rack shelves a couple of feet off the ground on one wall of your child's room so she can display treasures and enjoy them at her level.

❋ Attach a clothesline flat to the wall from one end to the other and hang pictures up with clothespins.

❋ Hang a large frame up on the wall. Put a plain colored piece of paper or board in the frame so it can serve as a backdrop to the artwork. Tape artwork to the front of the frame and change weekly.

❋ If you want the feel of a real art gallery, buy a few clip-on book lights to attach above paintings.

❋ Designate one shelf of storage as a show-and-tell space. Tell all the members of your family and friends to ask your child about the objects he places on this special shelf.

87

Stained Glass

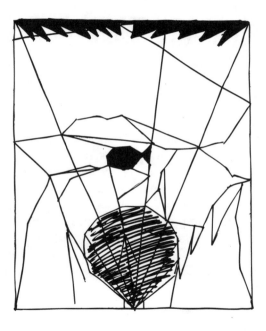

Age Range: 24 months and up

Make your own colorful window clings. Paint a sheet of cling wrap with markers, and then stick it to the window to see how the light streams through it. Or use two sheets to sandwich ripped pieces of colored tissue paper to form a beautiful mosaic. You can also use the cling wrap to mount artwork in the window, just make sure you have a thick enough "matte" of cling wrap around the picture to hold the artwork in place.

....

Words of Wisdom: *I have containers in the garage labeled by gender and size. I put outgrown children's clothes in them to save for future siblings, friends, and rummage sales. This also keeps the small bedroom closets from overflowing.*

—Jackie, Pocono Pines, Pennsylvania

88

You've Got Mail

Fashion a mailbox out of a shoe box, tissue box, milk carton, or oatmeal container. Paint or cover it in wrapping paper, contact paper, construction paper, pictures from children's catalogs, magazines, or comics. Personalize the mailbox with your child's name and add a flag. Attach the flag using a brass brad/paper fastener from the stationery store to allow it to swing up and down to signal when mail is waiting for pick-up. Keep it in your child's room (or just outside the door) and use the mailbox to unexpectedly deliver year-round valentines, thank-you notes, postcards, treats, and small toys.

Words of Wisdom: *My daughter absolutely loves it when I write her special notes. Even though she can't read them, she does recognize her name. I always draw a little picture or hearts and stars. She brings the note to me and I read it for her.*

—Beth, Grafton, Wisconsin

89

Room within a Room

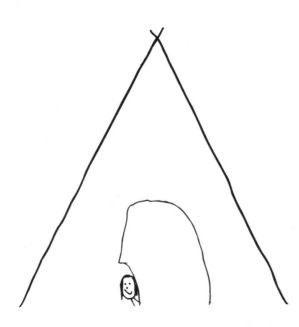

In a child's mind, even the smallest nook or cranny can become a hideaway, a fortress, or a teahouse. Create your child's own pint-sized private world ripe for imagination and exploration—or even just an afternoon snooze. Use a corner of her room to erect a small fabric tepee (canvas over PVC pipe, wooden dowels, or even bamboo sticks from a garden shop work great) or a circus tent out of a big colorful sheet or parachute. A playhouse can be fashioned from a giant appliance carton. Wallpaper or contact paper around the outside not only reinforces the cardboard structure for hours of door- and window-opening play, but also allows you to personalize it to your child's interests. Add carpet remnants to the floor, toss in fluffy pillows, make windows for peeking in and out, and use Velcro to attach a play phone to the inside wall. You'll "lose" your kid for hours!

90

Mini-Size It

When you're decorating your child's room, get down on his level and add some fun decorative touches. Make sure he can reach his toy storage bins and clothes.

* Install a second closet rod within reach. Hang a hat rack down low. Add a stepping stool.
* On your weekly grocery store trip, buy some inexpensive flowers for his room. Come home and arrange them in a vase together, and place them on a child-sized table. Replace the water and give them a fresh cut every day. It will make him feel important and in control of his surroundings as well as add a splash of color to his room.
* Make easy under-bed storage bins with wooden open-top boxes mounted on rolling casters from the hardware store. Make sure they're shallow enough to fit under the bed but hold enough to make them valuable. The kids can pull them out and load them up in no time!

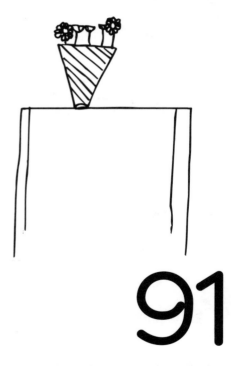

91

Lamp Shades

Age Range: 24 months and up

Novelty lamp shades are a great way to spruce up a room—and a cheap way to indulge what you know might be a passing obsession. Buy inexpensive, plain cardboard lamp shades and decorate them with felt-tipped markers or paint. You can even cut out favorite characters from magazines and decoupage them to the shade with decoupage medium and a sponge brush. Protect the finished product with matte acrylic varnish. These are easy to do—and redo—with passing fancies.

....

Words of Wisdom: *To make a bulletin board in my son's room, I covered a board with felt, and then stretched lengths of ribbon over the entire thing. I mounted it at his level so he could tuck items for display under the ribbons.*

—Wendy, Ramona, California

92

Felt Chains

Age Range: 30 months and up

Here is a twist to the old paper-doll chains we all used to make. Instead of using paper, make your chains out of felt. Take a yard of felt and cut it into strips lengthwise however tall you'd like your felt chain to be. Then fold it accordion-style and iron the edges as you go. Fold only as many squares at a time as you will be able to cut (felt, of course, is much thicker than paper). Any shape that has two connecting points will work: doll, elephant, angel, monkey, etc. You may want to use a stencil to draw the shape. Make sure to leave one point attached at both sides of the fabric or you will be left with individual objects instead of a chain. If you aren't sure how these chains work, experiment with paper first.

••

Words of Wisdom: *My daughter used to hate to wear hats, but now that I've put a hat rack in her room and allow her to choose her sun hat or winter hat, she is happy to wear one.*

—Marlene, Georgetown, Kentucky

93

Bed Headboards

Make them yourself!

* Use theme fabric, batting, and a staple gun to cover plywood for an upholstered look. Or paint a piece of canvas with an original design.
* Mount whitewashed fencing or lattice material to the wall for a picket-fence theme. Use thicker wood for a western look.
* Mount wooden baseball bats (you can drill right into them) as the slats for a headboard (you can buy the posts and center rail at a home center).
* Drape tulle from ceiling hooks or mosquito netting from a ring for a princess feel.

94

Section Two:
Playtime

Let's Get Physical

Scarf Play

Age Range: 15 to 18 months

Scarves are a must for any play box. Here are all the fun things you can do with them.

* Throw them in the air and watch them float down to the ground, then imitate the movements the scarf made while floating downward.
* Throw a bunch of them in the air and try to catch them as they float to the floor. Call out body parts while the scarves are in the air and try to catch them with those parts—"On your knees!" "Now on your nose!"
* Hold a scarf in each hand as you make big shapes in the air, then ask your child to copy the shapes you are making.
* Run with a scarf in each hand, letting the scarves flutter behind you.
* Make up an interactive dance of scarves as you wave your scarf around, over, and under your child as your child sits still on the floor. Switch positions.
* Tie the ends of the scarves together and stuff them into an old Kleenex box or paper-towel tube, then pull the scarves out.
* With the scarves tied together, wiggle them on the floor in a big side-to-side motion and ask your child to jump over the scarves as they move.

95

Rope Shapes

Materials
Rope of any kind

With a jump rope or length of cord, make a simple shape on the floor. Together, you and your child try to duplicate the shape with your bodies. Good shapes to try are rectangles, circles, straight lines, triangles, and curved or jagged lines. If other family members or other children are present, you may be able to do more complicated shapes, like letters or animals.

Words of Wisdom: *My son's favorite game before he learned to walk was for me to put a beanbag on his back while he crawled as fast as he could. I would mark how far he crawled before the beanbag fell off. He spent hours trying to beat his best mark.*
—Glenda, Holland, Michigan

96

Racing Game

Age Range: 18 months and up

Once a child learns to crawl or walk, all sorts of fun racing games are possible. Every race needs a starting line and a finish line. Don't forget to say, "On your mark, get set, go" before each race. Here are a few race ideas:

* Crawl on the floor pushing a beach ball in front of you with your head. The first one whose ball crosses the line wins.
* Lie on your side and roll to the finish line.
* Walk on tiptoes, hop, skip, jump, run, slide, or gallop.
* Put a beanbag on each of your backs as you crawl to the finish line.
* Each person puts on dress-up clothes before beginning. The first person to run over the finish line after putting the clothes on wins.

Words of Wisdom: *My son's absolute favorite indoor activity is to sit on a blanket or large beach towel and have me pull him around the house. This only works on our wood floors.*

—Eliza, Cooper City, Florida

97

Construction Zone

Age Range: 18 months and up

With a few big boxes, old blankets, and sheets, a city, spaceship, stage, or circus can be built. Clear a space inside or outside the house. Collect old blankets and sheets. Use the backs of couches, the swing set, outdoor furniture, or anything else you can find to drape the blankets over to create tent-like structures. If the furniture is cloth, you can use large safety pins to attach the blankets or sheets. You may even want to create a permanent fort-building supply box, including blankets and sheets that have slits cut in them one-half inch long, two inches away from the edge of the material. The slits will allow you to tie the sheets and blankets to various objects with string or ribbon.

98

Animal Play

Age Range: 18 months and up

Materials
Large paper grocery bags
Decorating supplies: colored construction paper, glue, fake fur, ribbons, yarn, paper streamers, paint, crayons, masking tape

It is much more fun to act like an animal if you look like one as well. Cut the paper bag up the front. Make a hole in the bottom of the bag for the head and holes for the arms so the bag fits like a jacket. Place the bag over the back of a chair so that it's easier to decorate. Decide what kind of animal you will be and then begin decorating. Your child might want to make up his own kind of animal, adding the trunk of an elephant to the black and white body of a zebra. Once the costumes are made, put them on and begin the animal dance. Move like your animal, make sounds, and pretend to eat and play like animals.

Mirror Dancing

Age Range: 21 to 24 months

Sit or stand in front of a large mirror. Begin your dance moving just your face and head. Help your child to move with you as he copies the movements you are making. Then raise your arms and move your legs as you encourage the same movements in your child. If your child raises her arm or turns in a circle, copy her. Once you've done this in the mirror for a while, turn to face each other. Now you will each be the mirror for each other. One person goes first making the movements as the other person follows. Switch so that each person has a chance to be the leader a few times.

....

Words of Wisdom: *My daughter says she doesn't like dancing to music...until I let her wear her "twirly dress." When we put that on, she'll dance like crazy for nearly an hour. After one of those dance sessions, she takes a wonderfully long afternoon nap!*

—Kealsy, North Bennington, Vermont

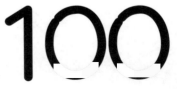

100

Indoor Baseball

Age Range: 21 to 36 months

It is possible to play baseball in the house without breaking anything. First you need to set up bases. The distance between them depends on the size of the room. You may want to change the rules so that the batter has to hop or crawl to the base after hitting the ball. Once the pitcher catches the hit ball, the pitcher has to run with the ball and touch the batter. Try using an inflated balloon or balled-up newspaper as a ball and an empty gift-wrap roll stuffed with newspaper as the bat. Of course, you'll also have to set up a location for batting practice. Attach a string to a soft ball, inflated balloon, or rolled-up newspaper. Hang the string with the ball falling at about your child's waist level from the ceiling or middle of a doorway. Show your child how to push the ball on the string and then try to hit it with the bat when the ball swings back.

101

Dance Fun

Age Range: 21 to 24 months

Hat dance: Hats come in all shapes and sizes, there are sun hats, hats with dog ears, pointed princess hats, cowboy hats, and Mexican sombreros. Put all your dress-up hats in a box. As you put each one on do a dance that matches the style of the hat.

Shake dance: Shout out different body parts for your child to shake. Let your child yell out body parts and watch you shake. Then shake together.

Flypaper dance: Attach contact paper to the floor with masking tape leaving the sticky side up. Now fly around the room like little flies. When you come to rest on the contact paper, dance frantically to escape being caught on the sticky flypaper.

102

Mattress Trampoline

Age Range: 24 months and up

Jumping is a favorite toddler activity. When your child has outgrown the crib, why not use the crib mattress on the floor as a trampoline? Make sure to move it away from the wall and put pillows around it just in case. Any kind of old mattress will work. Make up all sorts of bouncing games. Try to catch a ball in the air as you bounce, or go from feet to knees to bottom. Call out body parts to touch while in the air. Change facial expressions. Join hands and bounce together.

103

Freeze and Melt

Age Range: 24 to 30 months

This is a stop-and-go movement game with many variations. Have your child run freely around the room. When you say "freeze" she must stop and remain absolutely still. When you say "melt," your child can relax and start to move around again. Try the game again using music instead of your voice. Encourage your child to dance while the music is playing. When the music is turned off she freezes. When the music starts up she melts and begins to dance again. You can also make up other actions to follow the "freeze," like slow-motion. Other good action words to try might be "speed up," "down low," or "up high."

104

Chalk Town

Age Range: 24 to 30 months

Materials
Sidewalk chalk
Pavement or washable floor
Small cars and trucks
Cardboard
Blocks

Take the sidewalk chalk and draw a miniature town with roads, homes, a shopping center, school, airport, and gas station. Use the cardboard and blocks to make tunnels, bridges, and road signs. Drive the small cars and trucks around town, making sure to stop and visit each chalked location.

105

Masking Tape Work-Out

Age Range: 30 to 36 months

Kids love to move, wiggle, jump, roll, stamp their feet, and run in place. Set up a special work-out space for your child. Use masking tape to make shapes and lines on the floor or carpet. Have your child do some aerobic exercise in each space before following the line to the next shape. Make sure you get a work-out, too—let your child call out which activity you need to do when you get to the next space. Be sure to take off the tape when you're done playing, or the tape will get gooey and become nearly impossible to remove from carpeting.

106

Follow the Leader

Age Range: 30 to 36 months

Follow the leader is a fun game you can play every day. It lends itself to dozens of made up variations. Here are a few to try:

* Pretend to be spaceships, race cars, airplanes, bicycles, bulldozers, or fairies.
* Take turns leading, and ask each other to guess what you are before copying.
* Lead around the house or yard, introducing concepts like behind/in front, inside/outside, up/down, in/out, and left/right. Yell out the words as you do them.
* Act big and small, short and tall, loud and quiet. Use exaggerated voices to emphasize the difference—loud and booming for big, or quiet and squeaky for small.

107

Ball Play

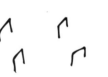

Balls a Rollin'

Age Range: 15 months and up

Young toddler's who aren't quite ready to catch a ball will enjoy these rolling games.

* Sit across from each other and roll the ball back and forth.
* Sit together and roll the ball into a goal that is set up across the room.
* Set up empty plastic soda bottles and roll the ball, trying to knock all the bottles over.
* Roll the ball out in front of the two of you, then have a crawling race to get the ball.
* Ask your child to lie on the floor on his stomach and roll the ball all over his body for a nice massage.
* Have your child lie on his side, making a crescent shape with his body. Roll the ball along the back and front of the crescent. Try making different shapes.

108

Parachute Ball

Age Range: 15 months and up

Materials
Old sheet, blanket, beach towel or play parachute
Balls of all sizes

If there are just two of you playing, use a beach towel. If more hands are available, use a sheet or parachute. Put a ball in the middle of the sheet, blanket, towel, or parachute. Have your child grab two corners and you grab two. If there are more people, ask them to hold edges of the material so that the ball doesn't fall off when it begins to roll. Get the ball rolling by lifting up one end of the fabric and then the other. Try raising the fabric up into the air quickly (and all together) to cause the ball to be propelled into the air, then try to catch the ball in the fabric as it falls. Lower the fabric all the way to the ground, then raise it high in the air. Let go of the fabric and hide so that the fabric and ball do not fall on top of you. Let your child lie on one end of the fabric, making sure that his head is clearly sticking out, then roll him up like a sausage. Once rolled up, hold the free end and let him roll out. Point out how he can also roll like a ball.

109

Tube Roll

Age Range: 18 months and up

Materials
Cardboard or plastic tubing (from poster shop or hardware store)
Masking tape
Small balls (large enough to avoid choking)

Use the different sizes and types of tubing to set up ball-roll games. Masking tape the tube to a chair and let the ball fall out into a basket. Tape a vertically leaning tube to a horizontal tube which is sitting on the floor to watch the ball roll out on the floor in the direction of a set target. Flexible tubing can be molded around objects, while clear tubing allows your child to watch the ball as it makes its way to the target location. If you have a stair rail, tie or tape the tubing to the rail and send the ball down the tube and into a bucket at the bottom of the stairs. Once tube construction begins, the design options are endless.

110

Balloon Tennis

Age Range: 18 months and up

Materials
Badminton racquet, ping-pong paddle, or cardstock in the shape of a paddle taped to a wooden spoon

Toddlers have such fun watching the cause and effect any kind of hitting action has on a balloon as it floats to the ceiling or over a net. First begin by hitting the balloon up toward the ceiling. Take turns hitting the balloon as it floats down. This will teach your child the idea that first one person hits it and then the other. Then tie a string between two kitchen chairs to act as a net. Stand on either side of the net close enough that when you hit the balloon, it will make it over the string. Use the same action of hitting the balloon upward and toward the other player, who will then hit the balloon back over the string.

111

Bumper Ball

Age Range: 18 months and up

Rolling lots of balls around an enclosed room, like a bathroom or kitchen, is exciting. Catching and pushing are only part of the fun—mostly it's watching all the balls bump into things and guessing what direction they might go next. Try standing on one end of the room and kicking the ball toward the side wall while you guess where the ball might ricochet and hit the other wall. Put an object in the middle of the room and see what happens when the ball collides with the object. Make sure the room you use is free of sharp corners so that your child will not reach down to pick up a ball and bang his head.

· ·

Words of Wisdom: *My mom always said a ball about the size of a child's head is just right—any bigger and it overwhelms, and any smaller and it's hard to control and balance.*

—Brett, Clarksville, Tennessee

112

Bedroom Basketball

Age Range: 24 months and up

Materials
Laundry basket
Sock, foam, or tennis balls

Place the laundry basket on top of a dresser for a game of basketball. Roll socks into balls, crunch up paper, or try a soft tennis ball. Try making a basket from different locations in the room. The lay-up shot includes taking two steps before shooting a basket from close range. The free throw might be from the head of the bed or some other distant location. Older kids can get into the action and play a game of "cow." One player shoots a basket from a specific location in the room. If the basket is good then the other player has to make a basket from that same location or he gets the letter "c." If both players make the basket from that location, the second player gets to choose a location to shoot the basket from. Whenever a player misses a basket that has been made by the player before him, another letter is added. Whoever spells the word "cow" first loses.

113

Big Ball Rolling

Age Range: 24 months and up

Materials
Large rubber ball (sold as exercise or physical-therapy balls)

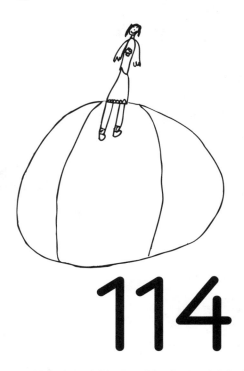

* Have your child lie across the top of the ball on his stomach, as you hold onto his ankles and rock him back and forth.
* Sit at least ten feet apart, facing each other. Push the ball back and forth with different body parts: your legs, heads, hands, elbows, or hips.
* Have your child lie across the top of the ball, face upward. This will give him a relaxing back stretch, but make sure he doesn't fall off the ball!
* Hold your child's hands as he sits on the ball and bounces up and down.
* Have him lie on the floor face down and roll the ball softly across his body.
* Have your child lie on his back on the floor with legs up in the air. Try balancing the ball on his feet. Encourage him to push the ball up in the air where you will catch it.

114

Frisbee Ball

Age Range: 24 months and up

Materials
Frisbee
Tennis ball

Turn the Frisbee over so that the ridge is pointing up. Place the tennis ball on the Frisbee and begin to roll the ball around the top. See how far you can tip the Frisbee without the ball rolling off. Make up an obstacle course or chalk line to follow while doing various motions with your body, like hopping, running, or jumping. Just walking and keeping the ball on the Frisbee can be a challenge! Have a Frisbee-roll competition. Each person has a Frisbee. See who can keep the ball rolling the longest before it falls off. Add other requirements like bending forward, lifting one leg up, making a happy face, or jogging in place.

115

Ball Pit

Age Range: 24 months and up

Make your child his own ball pit—it will be much cleaner and safer than the ones found at fast food restaurants or amusement parks! Get a large appliance box. Cut one side off the box and set it open-end up on the floor. Reinforce the edges with packing tape. Cut an entry door on one side of the box, making sure to stay above the ball line. Crawl in and enjoy the sensation of so many balls. Wiggle around until you reach the bottom, or roll around on the top for a mini massage.

Words of Wisdom: *My son developed a habit of throwing things—food off his tray, blocks against the wall, and toys onto the hardwood floors. But when we started making a conscious effort to play ball regularly, those exasperating behaviors slowed down dramatically. I guess our little pitcher just needed to exercise his throwing arm!*

—Peter, Suffolk, Virginia

116

Soccer

Age Range: 30 to 36 months

Materials
Sheet
Soft soccer ball

Pick the largest room in your home to set up an indoor soccer field. Take two kitchen chairs and set them seven feet apart. Use thick masking tape to attach a sheet to the floor between the chairs, then tie or tape the sheet to the chairs, creating a goal. Set cones or obstacles up around the room, or leave furniture where it is to act as obstacles. Begin on one side of the room kicking the ball, running around the obstacles until the goal is in sight. Once your child has had a few practice runs against the stationary obstacles, you might want to stand in as goalie, trying to block her shot. Switch roles.

117

Bouncy-Ball Book

Age Range: 30 to 36 months

Together select magazine pages with interesting images. Cut them out and glue them onto a piece of construction paper. Give your child one brightly colored dot sticker to place somewhere on each page. Then make a construction paper cover and bind all the pages together with ribbon, string, or staples. Look through the book and find the ball on every page. Flip quickly through the book and watch the ball bounce. You can also make a bouncy-ball book with an old picture book.

••

Words of Wisdom: *My brother told me that toddlers have a tendency to go through a throwing stage, so my wife and I taught our daughter to always toss a ball underhanded so it would stay low to the ground and roll without hurting anyone or anything.*

—Victoria, Roland, Arizona

118

Tunnel Fun

Age Range: 30 to 36 months

First create several tunnels using boxes, chairs, tables, or human legs. Set up a course the ball will roll through. Make a mark on the floor where the ball will begin, then push the ball toward the first tunnel. When the ball comes out on the other side, push it along the course to the next tunnel. You may want to begin the tunnel course with a flat piece of cardboard acting as a ramp for the ball to roll down. Be creative and look around the house for other objects to add to your tunnels of fun.

• •

Words of Wisdom: *I always deflate our beach balls just enough to make them easier for my son to grab and catch.*
—Kate, Virginia Beach, Virginia

119

Croquet

Age Range: 30 months and up

Materials
Wiffle balls
Long-handled wooden spoons
Bricks, boxes, or books

Use bricks, boxes, or books to create a croquet course. Each person needs a ball and a wooden spoon. Adults must play this game while on their knees. Decide which pathway the ball has to go through first. Take turns hitting your own ball until it makes it through the created pathway. When the ball does make it through the pathway, that player gets an extra turn. If by chance a ball is hit by another ball, the hit player must put her ball back on the other side of the pathway. This is a great introduction to turn-taking as well as understanding and creating rules.

120

Art and Sculpture

Cleaning Arsenal

Stock up on all the things you'll need to keep the house in shape when your artists get out of hand!

- WD-40 gets crayon off of painted walls. Spray it into a rag and rub gently onto the crayon-marked surface. Wait a few minutes and wipe it away. Then you'll need to wash the oil up with either a small amount of window cleaner or water with a tiny amount of dishwashing liquid. Test in an inconspicuous place first.
- Use the same technique outdoors if your child has used crayon instead of sidewalk chalk on your sidewalk, patio, or brickwork—only you'll need a bristle brush and some manpower on those!
- A cotton ball doused in rubbing alcohol will remove most marker stains from household surfaces. Soft Scrub will also do the trick for many a marker mishap.
- Hairspray, glycerin, and alcohol can also remove ink stains from fabrics.
- Dry baking soda and a small brush (try an old toothbrush) gets crayon, pencil, and ink out of upholstery.
- Enzyme cleaners, also known as digestives, "eat" protein stains like grass, blood, and egg yolk.

121

Moving Masterpiece

Age Range: 15 months and up

Materials

Tempera paint   Pie tin or clean Styrofoam tray
Newspapers
Large pieces of paper: butcher paper, newsprint, the backside of unused wallpaper,
      wrapping paper
Ball: tennis ball, golf ball, baseball (lightweight plastic balls will not roll with paint
      on them)

Choose an area that's easy to clean up, like the floor, patio, garage, or deck. Spread newspapers on the work surface, and place the paper on top. Set the ball in the paint and roll it around a little before setting it on the paper and rolling it to your child. Make sure you instruct your toddler to roll the ball on the paper. Your adventurous child might try bouncing the ball on the paper, so beware. It's also fun to dip the wheels of a favorite plastic or wooden vehicle in the paint and zoom it across the paper.

....

Words of Wisdom: *I add a few drops of dishwashing liquid to tempera paint. It makes it easier to wash hands and clothes.*
—Kimberly, Beverly, Massachusetts

122

Flour Prints

Age Range: 15 months and up

Materials
Container with water
Construction paper
Flour
Shellac
Towel

Have your child dip his hand or feet into the container of water. Shake off any excess water. Place her hand or foot on top of the construction paper, making sure to lift it on and off so it makes a clear water print. Ask her to step onto the towel while you sprinkle flour onto the wet spots on the construction paper. Let the wet flour dry, then spray or paint it with shellac. Try making interesting patterns on the paper, but always dip hands or feet into the water and shake them before making the next print.

123

Bag Painting

Age Range: 15 months and up

Materials
Large Ziploc bag
Finger paint

Put the finger paint inside the bag. If using more than one color of finger paint, space the paint blobs so there is room for the paint to squish without overlapping. Rub your hand over the top of the bag to flatten out the paint. Let your child make pictures by pushing on the paint with a fingertip until the paint gives way to a clear line. To change the background color, put different colors of construction paper or pictures from magazines underneath the bag.

Words of Wisdom: *We didn't have the floor space or budget for a store-bought easel, so we made our own wall easel by using two large cup hooks to hold up a one-inch-diameter dowel (cut about eight to ten inches wider than our roll of craft paper).*
—Jasmine, Rising Sun, Maryland

124

Print Magic

Age Range: 18 months and up

Materials

Flat sponges   Potatoes
Washable liquid paint   Paper
3 flat pans or plates to put paint in

Sponge prints: Cut the sponge into one geometric shape of different sizes. For example, do squares and make them small, medium, and large. Pour colored paints into three flat containers and put a sponge in each. Help your child to dip the sponge in the paint and then press it onto the paper. Make any design you want. Once the paint has dried, cut the sheet of paper into the geometric shape you used. Take a walk around, inside or outside, and, holding up the shaped piece, find other things that are the same shape.

Potato Prints: Cut the potato in half. Use a knife to cut out a design on the potato. Whatever is raised will be seen on the print. Place a sponge in the paint. Press the potato onto the paint-soaked sponge, then press the potato onto the paper. Wash the potato off if another color is used, and keep printing.

125

Clay Works

Age Range: 21 months and up

Go to your nearest art supply store and buy a big bag of clay. Clay feels different from play dough. It is much denser and is slippery when water is applied. You can sculpt it with your hands, or use rocks, sticks, or wooden clay tools. Using a string held taut between your hands or a butter knife, remove a chunk of clay from the bag. An old pillowcase makes a good surface on which to model; it can be folded up afterward and used each time the clay is brought out. Fill a small container with water and show your child how to dip fingertips into the water, rubbing them on the clay. Pinch the clay to make shapes. The clay will dry hard if left out for a few days and can be painted, but it will also be very breakable. Make sure to display the sculpted pieces.

126

Super-Stretch Dough

Age Range: 21 to 24 months

Materials
2 bowls and plastic container with lid
2 cups Elmers glue
1½ cups water
Food coloring
⅓ cup water (2 times)
1 teaspoon borax (2 times)

Mix Elmers glue, several drops of food coloring, and 1½ cups water in a bowl. In the other bowl, mix ⅓ cup water with the borax, then stir it into the glue mixture. A blob will form that you pull out and place in a plastic container. Knead it slightly. To the remaining glue mixture add water and borax again. Stir and pull out another blob, combining it with the first in the plastic container. You now have a dough that can go the distance. Stretch, loop, spiral, braid, wiggle, cut, roll, and spread. Watch what happens if you leave it on the table in a ball for just a few minutes.

127

Wallpaper Drawing

Age Range: 21 to 24 months

Most kids find a way to write on the walls one way or another, so why not give them a space where writing on the wall becomes a form of art? Tape a big piece of butcher paper to the wall. Tie a long string around individual crayons and then tape the crayons to the top of the paper. That way, whenever the urge hits to draw, your child can pick up a crayon and continue the wallpaper design. Draw a scene or scribble with your child. Encourage the rest of the family to contribute to the design.

Words of Wisdom: *One day my husband was watching our daughter while he was watching a football game. She wrote all over the walls with crayon. He had just finished fixing the door hinges, so he tried the WD-40 on the walls, and it erased our new crayon drawings right away!*

—Jessica, Walnut Creek, California

128

Spin Painting

Age Range: 21 to 24 months

Materials
Salad spinner
Tempera paints
Variety of paper, coffee filters, comics

Take the inner strainer out of the salad spinner. Place a piece of paper or coffee filter at the bottom of the bowl. Put the strainer back in. Put one teaspoon each of different colored tempera paints in the bottom of the strainer. Put the lid on. Show your child how to spin the salad spinner. Once you've spun it around twenty times, stop and take the inner strainer out to see the beautiful piece of spin art you've created. Experiment with color combinations and different kinds of paper.

Words of Wisdom: *If you want to make a really cool paint pen, take the top off an empty bottle of roll-on deodorant and fill it with liquid tempera paint, then roll away!*
—Bonnie, Newport Beach, California

129

Foil with Oil

Age Range: 24 months and up

Materials
Baby oil
Tinfoil or wax paper
Small pieces of art tissue paper (not facial tissue)

Cut or tear tissue paper into small pieces. Tear off a piece of foil or wax paper as large as the piece of art will be. Squeeze a drop or two of oil onto the foil. Place one of the tissue paper pieces on top. The paper will stick, but it is not permanent. Layer the tissue paper to create a collage using different colors for contrast. This is a great sensory experience, and it smells nice, too.

• •

Words of Wisdom: *Once a month when my house seems taken over with kids' artwork, I take photos or videotape of the kids next to their creations. Then when I throw some of them away, I don't feel so bad.*
—Renee, Hendersonville, Tennessee

130

Painter's Paradise

Age Range: 24 to 30 months

Cling wrap painting: Drop globs of paint onto a piece of paper. Put a piece of cling wrap over the paper and rub the paint around under it.
Blow painting: Add water to tempera paint so that it is a bit runny. Put drops of paint on the paper and blow it with a straw, creating various designs.
Ice-cube painting: Put a piece of paper in a large, rectangular cake pan. Sprinkle powdered tempera paint onto the paper. Put an ice cube in the pan and let it melt a bit before moving the pan from side to side, allowing the ice-cube trail to create the design.

Try using different kinds of objects to paint with: popsicle sticks, cotton balls and swabs, feathers, spoons, and sponges.

Words of Wisdom: *It's amazing what you can find around the house to use in paint printing. My granddaughter loves using a toothbrush, berry basket, corks, whisks, cookie cutters, and toilet paper tubes.*
—Sara, Playa Del Rey, California

131

Event Wreath

Age Range: 24 months and up

Kids love to collect pictures, souvenirs, tickets, leaves, or anything they can find to take home with them when they go someplace special. Next time you go on a nature walk, take a trip to the beach, or go visit grandma make sure to bring back little reminders of your trip. Purchase a Styrofoam wreath at a craft store. Have your child paint the wreath. Attach your treasures with glue, florist tape, or wire. Let your child help create the design and where each item will be attached. Hang the wreath in a prominent place in your home so everyone can admire your child's handiwork.

....

Words of Wisdom: *My daughter didn't like wearing an art smock, but I didn't like washing her stained clothes when she didn't wear one. So we purchased a canvas apron and used fabric paint to stamp her handprints all over it in several colors. Now she loves to cover up!*

—Jill, Pompey, New York

132

Antique Vase

Age Range: 30 to 36 months

Materials

Masking tape

Decorative bottle or vase

Brown shoe polish

Soft cloth

Kids like the sticky feel of masking tape. Some kids might be able to rip the tape into little pieces, but for those whose fingers aren't quite as coordinated, rip the masking tape for them into one-to-two–inch pieces. Put the ripped pieces around the top of any kind of container so that they can be easily grabbed. You will be covering the decorative bottle or vase completely with these little pieces of tape. Once there is no glass showing, let your child use the brown shoe polish over the tape. Before the polish dries use a soft cloth to wipe it off, leaving an antique look. This project is great for gift-giving.

Words of Wisdom: *If you want some beautiful art and drawing paper, go to a local printer and ask if you can leave a box for them to put the week's scraps in. It saves the environment and gives your child unusual supplies to work with.*

—Bridgett, Overland Park, Kansas

133

Fashion Design

Age Range: 30 to 36 months

Materials
Sheet of craft or butcher paper
Markers
Fabric scraps, ribbons, and yarn
Glue

Have your little one lie down on a giant piece of craft or butcher paper. Trace her body with a big marker. Armed with colorful markers, fabric scraps, ribbons, and yarn, let her design an outfit. You may want to help glue the fabric down once she places it where she wants it. This is also a fun way to design a costume you might want to make for a special event. This way you get to see what the finished product might look like and make changes in advance.

134

Pot Painting

Age Range: 30 to 36 months

Use masking tape to make horizontal and/or vertical stripes along a terra cotta garden pot. Let your child paint the pot with acrylic paints. Remove the tape when the paint dries and see how delighted he is to see that he created such tidy, symmetrical work. Later, protect the painted finish from the elements with a coat or two of polyurethane varnish. These make great daycare-provider or grandparent gifts, especially when you fill them with an herb or flower.

Words of Wisdom: *Whenever we give gifts to grandparents or teachers, I ask my son to tell me all the things he can remember about that person, as well as the things they've done together, or what he likes about them. I write it down exactly as he says it, then put it in a card to go with the gift.*

—Fran, Half Moon Bay, California

135

Game Time

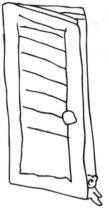

Container Magic

Age Range: 15 months and up

Materials
3 or 4 colored large plastic bowls
Small toys

Put the bowls face down on the floor. Place a small toy under one of the bowls. Make sure your child sees which bowl the toy is placed under. Then move the containers around, sliding them on top of the hard surface, as if in a magic act. Once you've moved the bowls around for a while, have your child guess which container the toy is hiding under.

136

Magnet Mystery

Age Range: 15 months and up

Materials
Metal cookie sheet or cake pan
Magnets

Kids love to play with magnets—maybe it is the slight resistance of pulling them off metal or the way they jump to stick back onto metal. Collect a variety of magnets or buy a sheet of flat magnets and glue pictures or objects onto them. Make up stories with the magnets. Have your child sort the magnets into similar groupings. Buy a set of alphabet magnets and begin to make words. Simply taking the magnets on and off a cookie sheet or sliding them around is entertaining. Have your child cover his eyes, then take one away and ask which magnet is missing. Best of all, there is no mess and all the pieces stick together for carrying.

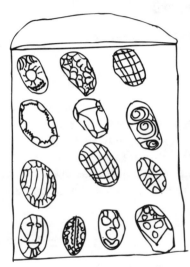

137

Penny Waterfall Game

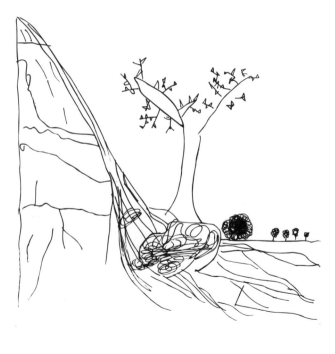

Age Range: 18 to 21 months

Materials
Container
A bag of pennies

Here's a fun game that everyone in the family can participate in. Fill a container almost to the top with water. Give each player a pile of pennies. Go around the circle and have each player take a turn putting one penny into the container. The player whose penny makes the water overflow loses the game. You can also play this game using dice. Roll the dice, and whatever number the player gets determines how many pennies are to be put in the container.

138

Paper Pull

Age Range: 21 months and up

Materials
Construction paper
Stapler or glue

Make a bunch of construction-paper chains and then, on the count of three, do a gentle tug of war with them—the winner is the one who holds the most loops when it breaks. Continue grabbing the remaining chains and counting again before doing a tug of war. Keep doing this until there are no more linked chains.

· ·

Words of Wisdom: *My son gets upset when he doesn't always win, but of course he can't always win— especially when he plays with his peers. One thing we do is periodically change, during an activity, what winning is. Sometimes the long straw wins, and other times the short straw wins.*

—Charlie, Lumpkin, Georgia

139

Object Outline

Age Range: 21 to 24 months

Materials
Paper, pencil
Small objects: spoon, key, cookie cutter, etc.

Put each object on a piece of paper and draw an outline around it. Place all the pieces of paper with outlined items into a big box. Place all the real objects in another box or on the counter. Give your child the box of outlined items. Ask him to place the real object on top of the drawn matching outline. A harder version of this game is to put all the real objects back where they belong. Then cut the paper object outlines into individual cards and give your child a particular card. Ask him to go find the object that was outlined.

140

Go Get It

Age Range: 21 months and up

Ask your child to find a variety of objects. You might ask her to find one object at a time or a few similar items at a time. For instance, you might ask for a pink toy or a favorite bear. Then ask for an item from the kitchen, followed by a ball of some kind. As your child brings you each object, put it in a pile behind a couch, so your child can't see it. Once all the items are hiding behind the couch, take one of the items and put it into a big bag. Have your child close her eyes and reach into the bag to feel the object. Encourage her to tell you what the object is that she is feeling without opening her eyes to look at it.

141

Channel Surfing

Age Range: 21 months and up

Kids love playing with remote controls. Find an old remote control. Make sure the batteries are removed. Tell your child to push the buttons. When she does, change your facial expression. Every time she presses a button, change your facial expression again. When she realizes that by pushing the remote control she's changing your channels, expand the charade to include various body poses. Switch roles, and ask her to make faces or poses while you push the buttons.

142

Sensory Guess What

Age Range: 24 months and up

This game can be played with food or other items that have a distinct smell. Either blindfold your child or have him close his eyes. Then set the items one at a time in front of him. Use touch, taste, and smell as you encourage your child to guess what each item is. On the taste tests, simply put the food near your child's nose and mouth and let him taste if he wants to. For items that you wouldn't taste, like a blouse that smells like mom's favorite perfume, a dog toy, or your child's favorite blanket, let your child hold the items and put them up to his own nose to sniff. Switch roles and let your child do the taste and smell test on you.

143

What's Missing

Age Range: 24 to 30 months

Put six to ten objects on a tray. Let your child look at the tray, pick up each object, and tell you the name of the object. Then ask your child to turn around while you remove one object. Then ask her to tell you what is missing from the tray. Give her clues if she has a hard time remembering what is missing. Switch roles. Put more objects on the tray when an adult is guessing what is missing!

....

Words of Wisdom: *My son's favorite game is to pull a helium balloon down from the ceiling and then let it go and watch it float back up. He'll do this for quite a while. It's even more fun if there are many balloons so he can run back and forth pulling them at different times.*

—Carl, Memphis, Tennessee

144

Letter Fishing

Age Range: 30 to 36 months

Materials
Old business cards
Paper clips
Box
String
Magnet

Write a letter, number, or shape on one side of each business card. Attach a paper clip to the top of the cards. Put the cards in a large box, face up. Make a fishing pole out of the string and magnet. Call out a letter, number, or shape and have your child fish for it.

....

Words of Wisdom: *My daughter used to cry endlessly when I left her at daycare, until the teacher suggested I give her a bottle of the lotion I wear. Now when she misses me she asks the teacher if she can rub some of that lotion on her hands and she feels better.*

—Sarah, Liberal, Kansas

Bead Catcher

Age Range: 30 to 36 months

Materials
Plastic scoop from a large box of detergent
String or ribbon 8 inches long
1-inch bead
$\frac{1}{2}$-inch bead

Poke a hole in the bottom of the plastic scoop. Thread the string or ribbon through the hole in the scoop. Tie the $\frac{1}{2}$-inch bead to the string so it can't slip back through the hole. Tie the one-inch bead to the other end of the string. Show your child how to swing the bead up and around in the air to be caught in the scoop. Make one for yourself as well so you can play together. If your child is not coordinated enough to catch the bead in the cup, set up small plastic figures or blocks; then, have your child hold the scoop above the figures and swing the bead as she tries to knock them over.

146

Puzzle Hunt

Age Range: 30 to 36 months

Select a simple puzzle. Take the pieces apart and hide them around the room. Write down the number of pieces that are hidden. Hunt together for all the pieces before completing the puzzle together.

· ·

Words of Wisdom: *I read a great article in* Mothering *magazine that recommended letting your child have the tantrum without trying to squelch him/her, but making sure that you're close by, so that your child knows you're "there." It's worked quite well—her tantrums don't seem to last that long. One time, she insisted on rolling around the hard kitchen floor. When I offered her a pillow for her head, she said, "Yeah," and then she just spent a little time lying on the floor. Then it was over.*

—Jane, Novato, California

147

Go Fish

Age Range: 30 months and up

Make twelve or more pairs of cards by hand or on the computer using recognizable animals, shapes, colors, or family members. Laminate the cards with contact paper for a longer-lasting game. Mix them up and deal three cards apiece. To play Go Fish, you begin by asking the other player for a card you need to make a pair. If the player doesn't have it he says, "Go fish," and you pick a card from the pile. The first person to match all of the cards in his hand wins.

148

Hand Measurer

Age Range: 36 months and up

Here's a fun way to introduce the concept of measurement to your child. Trace your child's hand and foot on a sturdy piece of cardboard or felt. Do the same with your foot and hand. Cut them out. Decorate them however you would like. Show your child how to measure an object using his hand or foot as measurement. For example, the kitchen rug might be eight of your child's hands and five of his feet. See how many hands and feet it takes to measure a variety of objects. Once your child has measured something, take out your own hand and foot cutouts and measure them again. Try guessing how many feet or hands an object might be before you measure it.

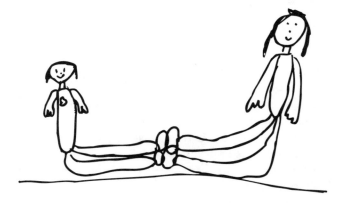

149

Memory Games

Age Range: 36 months and up

Photo match: Whenever you get pictures developed, make sure to get duplicate copies so you can use them for this matching memory game. You might also want to take a special roll of pictures of individual objects, the family pet, family members, or friends that your child will recognize. Place ten to twenty pictures face down on the floor, making sure there is a match for each photo. Turn the photos over two at a time, trying to remember where the match is. As each player finds matching pictures, the pictures are taken off the floor and put in a pile next to that player. Whoever has the most matches at the end wins.

What's in the picture?: Use photographs or pictures cut from magazines for this game. Give your child the picture. Ask him to look at it for a few minutes. Then take the picture and ask one simple question like, "Is there a dog in the picture?"; "Who has red hair?"; "How many cats did you see?"; "What color was Grandma wearing?"; or "Did Grandpa have glasses on?" If he answers it correctly, ask another—if incorrectly, laugh it up!

150

Where's It Hiding?

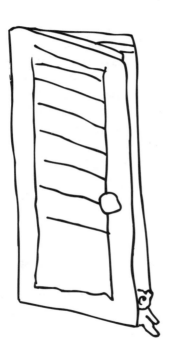

Age Range: 21 to 24 months

Tie a very long string around your child's favorite stuffed animal or doll. Place the toy in a hiding place in the child's room or somewhere in the house. Now take the string and run it over and under furniture and around other objects in the room. Give your child the end of the string. Tell him to follow the string to the hiding place of his favorite stuffed animal or doll. This is also fun to do with a present or surprise tied to the end of the string.

151

Music and Songs

Silly Sing-Along

Age Range: 15 months and up

Putting new words to a favorite tune is an easy way to help your child focus on daily activities. For instance, "The Wheels on the Bus" can be adapted to "This is the way we brush our teeth…before we go to bed." Your child will more happily comply and you'll find her singing along. You can also make up silly words to go with familiar tunes to make you both laugh.

....

Words of Wisdom: *With my first child, I couldn't remember any songs or nursery rhymes, so I typed them up one day and hung them by the changing table, in the kitchen, and other places where I might like to sing. Now I just look at the words while I sing until I know them.*

—Susan, Culver City, California

152

Parade

Age Range: 15 months and up

Marching around the house in a single file line followed by a parent, brother, sister, or pulled toy is a favorite game for all toddlers. The joy of newfound freedom in walking, marching, or hopping to music is a highlight of the parade experience. Consider dressing up to go along with a specified theme of perhaps clowns, animals, or fairies. Play toy instruments or make your own musical sounds. Play music with a distinct rhythm and then try to march on beat. Make sure to videotape the parade so your child can watch his production later.

153

World Music

Age Range: 15 months and up

Expose your child to different kinds of music: African, Brazilian, French, Italian, Gregorian chant, or classical, to name a few. Find a children's song tape in a foreign language with simple songs that repeat, and then learn one or two. Look for music with unusual rhythms and moods so you can dance to a different beat. Make sure to pull out a world map and point to the country where the music originated. It is also fun to find a book at the library about that country so your child can see how the people dress, live, and play.

....

Words of Wisdom: *We sing songs in the car when I want to keep my daughter awake—there's nothing worse than having her drift off just before we get home for nap-time or bedtime.*

—Trisha, Bayfield, Wisconsin

154

Rubber-Band Harp

Age Range: 18 months and up

Materials
Several rubber bands of many sizes and thicknesses
Facial-tissue box
Pencil
Cardboard tube
Newspaper

Stretch the rubber bands across the tissue box. Put the pencil underneath the rubber bands just to the side of the hole. Fill the cardboard tube with scrunched up newspaper to make it stronger. Cut a hole in the end of the tissue box just big enough to fit the cardboard tube—now you have a guitar handle. Tape the tube firmly in place. Pluck the bands with your fingers and listen to the different sounds. Try holding the rubber band in the middle and plucking. What happens to the sound? Also, try strumming your fingers across all of the bands. Your child will have fun pulling and letting go as long as the bands are not so close together that he gets his fingers pinched.

155

Ribbon Dancing

Age Range: 18 months and up

Children move to music naturally. They will quicken or slow their pace according to the musical mood. Give them a chance to be the director of a shower of ribbons as the ribbons dance to the music. Tie three or four ribbons to a plastic shower-curtain ring. Make enough rings so that each child has two, one for each hand. Prepare a variety of songs, from classical to blues. While the music is playing, hold the rings and move the ribbons to the mood of the music. Tell a story with the ribbons as they move through the air. Wiggle them quickly to show excitement, or let them float to the floor in calm. Encourage your child to put her whole body into it.

156

Musical Fingers

Age Range: 18 months and up

Set out a large piece of paper along with finger paints of various colors. Play different kinds of music and encourage your child to finger paint to it, picking the color that best reflects each kind of music and painting to the rhythm, tempo, or emotion expressed. Paint alongside your child, tapping the paper quickly to the staccato beats and letting your hand gracefully sweep the page on the slow, soft melodies. Get both your hands into the action. Feel the movement of the paint as an extension of the music. Keep adding more paint when needed.

157

Head, Shoulders, Knees and Toes

Age Range: 21 months and up

Toddlers are interested in body parts. A great way to help them learn the names of body parts or to show how proud they are that they already know them is to sing a song where they can act out their newfound knowledge. Here are two favorites:

Head, shoulders, knees, and toes.
Knees and toes.

Head, shoulders, knees, and toes.
Knees and toes.

Eyes and ears and mouth and nose,
Head, shoulders, knees, and toes.
Knees and toes.

If you're happy and you know it clap your hands (physically clap hands)
If you're happy and you know it clap your hands (physically clap hands)
If you're happy and you know it, then your face would surely show it,
If you're happy and you know it clap your hands.
(stomp your feet, turn around, shout hurray, shake your head, etc.)

158

Homemade Instruments

Age Range: 24 months and up

All sorts of instruments can be made out of materials found around the house.

Paper-plate tambourines: Staple or tape two paper plates together, leaving a space to pour in some dried beans. Staple or tape closed.

Maracas: Fill a plastic container with dried beans or pasta and shake.

Drums: Tape a few empty oatmeal containers together to create a bongo drum, or tie a string around one to make a marching drum.

Horns: Find different-sized funnels and blow through them to make the sound of a horn.

Cymbals: Hit spoons together or against a metal lid.

Blocks: Put sandpaper on one side of two blocks, and have your child rub them together.

Words of Wisdom: *We have a clean-up song—whenever I start humming it, my son knows it's time to start picking up his toys.*
—Jessica, Robinson, Illinois

159

Clapping Rhythms

Age Range: 24 to 30 months

Clapping is a fun way for kids to participate in any musical endeavor. In its simplest form, a clapping game begins when one person claps a rhythm and the other tries to copy it. It is also fun to listen to familiar songs and clap along with them or tap your hands on the floor or your knees, and stomp your feet to the beat. You might ask your child to create the rhythm of a dance by clapping her hands in whatever rhythm she likes while you dance to that rhythm. Partner hand-clapping games are also fun. Sit across from each other. Make up a clapping pattern to include hands clapping straight across, then crossing in the middle or hitting your legs. The idea is to make the pattern simple enough for your child to follow and then repeat it a few times.

160

Kitchen Band

Age Range: 24 months and up

The kitchen offers endless musical possibilities: pans turned upside-down, plastic containers hit with wooden spoons, a wire whisk lightly strumming a roasting rack, spoons hitting spoons. Sit on the floor with various containers, bowls, pans, and utensils spaced around you and your child. Put on some music and play along with it, hitting the kitchen instruments like you would a drum set. Have other family members pick up one of the instruments and play together. Let your child play as you make dinner or do other kitchen work.

• •

Words of Wisdom: *Glue nickels, pennies, and quarters onto the bottom of an old pair of shoes to make tap shoes. Let your child try these fun shoes out on cement or a piece of flooring that is already scuffed.*

—Jason, Cadillac, Michigan

161

Guess the Noise

Age Range: 30 to 36 months

Here's a game that can be played anywhere. It will teach your child to listen carefully and become more sensitive to sounds. Have your child shut his eyes and guess the sounds you are making. Here are a few ideas:

Kitchen: water dripping, fork on the sink, fork on a glass or pan, putting a lid on a pan, refrigerator door opening, or microwave bell

Around the house: ball bouncing on the floor, phone dialing or ringing, or a door closing

Container rattles: Put different things into containers to see what they sound like—rice versus beans versus popcorn versus tissue, etc. Then show your child what you are going to put into the container and ask him to guess what it might sound like before actually trying it. Take turns. Ask your toddler to make the sounds while you guess.

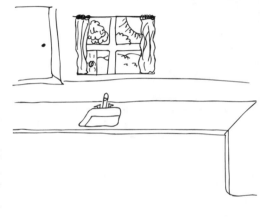

162

Sound Count

Age Range: 30 to 36 months

Here's a musical game that helps your child learn his numbers. Roll a die. Whatever number shows up on the die determines the number of sounds your child needs to make. These sounds can be made by clapping, humming, singing, or playing various musical instruments. The fun of this game comes in stringing the various sounds together as the non–sound making participant counts. Take turns. Help your child count the number of sounds by saying a number as his sound is made.

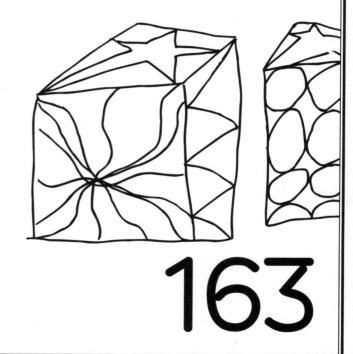

163

Story Soundtrack

Age Range: 36 months and up

Pick a favorite storybook that happens to have action that might be associated with a certain sound like rain, footsteps, wind, train whistles, or crackling fire. Or write your own story with some of these elements. To create rain, spray water from the sink sprayer into a bowl of water or run the shower into a bucket. For footsteps, go outside and walk on gravel, or fill a box with sand or gravel and walk in place. Create the sound of running the same way. For the sound of a fire, crumple up an empty potato-chip bag. You can purchase train whistles in hobby stores. Be creative with all the sounds you can create. Record the sounds in the order you would hear them in the book. Then, as each sound is read, you can turn on the tape. It is also fun to have the sound-effect makers right at hand so you can add them live as the story is read.

164

Imaginative Play

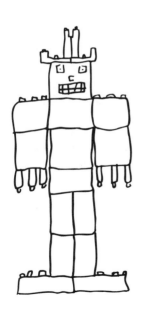

Puppet Play

Age Range: 15 months and up

Start a puppet collection. Keep them in a special container so they can be pulled out to enact a story you're reading or thrown in the car to entertain on long car rides.

Sock puppets: Find an old sock. Use pieces of felt and fabric paint to create a character at the toe of the sock.

Popsicle stick puppets: Use construction paper or magazine images to create a face and body for your puppet. Glue your character to a piece of cardboard and then attach it to a Popsicle stick.

Finger puppets: Use an old glove to make a family of joined finger puppets, or cut the fingers off of the glove to create individual characters. Use felt and paint or permanent markers to decorate.

Mask puppets: Draw a face on a paper plate. Cut out the eyes, nose, and mouth. Decorate with hair, glasses, a mustache, or whatever suits your character. Glue the mask to a wooden dowel so you can hold it in front of your face when you talk.

165

Balloon Friends

Age Range: 15 months and up

Children are intrigued with balloons. Inflate a few balloons. Use permanent markers to make faces on them. Give each balloon a specific expression, name, and character trait. Attach a string or a stick. Introduce your child to the balloon with a formal introduction, "Suzy, I'd like you to meet Slick Mick, the boy who likes to do tricks." Then let your child watch as you act out the part of each balloon. Let your child join in by becoming one of the characters. Remember to dispose of the balloon when you are finished playing. Deflated balloons or pieces of a popped balloon are choking hazards.

166

My One Block

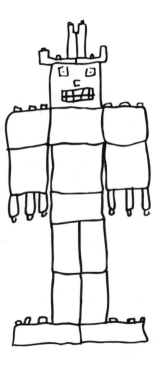

Age Range: 18 months and up

The joy of childhood is in the ability to see the extraordinary in the ordinary. Pick out a few of the blocks your child likes to play with. Paint or decorate them in a special way that sets them apart from the other blocks. Tell your child that these blocks are make-believe blocks. These special blocks can become dogs as you push them along the floor, airplanes raised overhead, or perhaps circus trains traveling into town. Maybe the blocks are people, animals, or magic fairies. Enter into this imaginative play world with your child—enjoy the magic of make believe.

167

Everyday Play Dough

Age Range: 18 months and up

Play dough is not just for squishing and rolling. It can help to tell a story. Think up a story you'd like to tell your child. Then take a piece of play dough and mold it into a shape of something related to the story. (The idea is to use your imagination, so the shape doesn't have to look exactly like what you're describing.) As the story continues and new characters emerge, encourage your child to pick up the play-dough shape and mold it into something else. It is also fun to make many shapes, one for each character, before the story begins.

Below is a recipe for smooth, pliable dough. It can be stored in a plastic container for several weeks, and does not need to be refrigerated.

Saucepan
2 cups flour
1 teaspoon cream of tartar
1 teaspoon food coloring
1 cup salt
2 tablespoons oil
2 cups water

Mix all ingredients in the saucepan, stirring constantly, over medium heat until dough leaves the sides of the pan. Continue to stir the dough ball around in the pan for a minute, then remove it from the pan and knead it for several minutes.

168

Dress-Up Box

Age Range: 21 months and up

Today is a great day to start a dress-up box for your child. Go through your closet and, instead of discarding your old clothes, look for things that would make good dress-up items. Old scarves, jewelry, high-heeled shoes, jackets, dresses, purses, and blouses. Visit antique and thrift shops for old dresses. Tell your friends that you're collecting old bridesmaid's dresses—the ones that will never be worn again. Make sure to put a full-length mirror up so your child can see the full effect. It's also fun to save old makeup to bring out for special occasions. Make sure to have your video camera out the first time your daughter tries to make-up her own face!

Words of Wisdom: *Big scarves are my daughter's favorite playtime accessories. We dance with them, make costumes, tie them together to connect us like train cars, play peek-a-boo with them, and more. I even carry a few in my diaper bag.*

—Margaret, Asheville, North Carolina

169

Mail Play

Age Range: 21 months and up

Whenever you are out and about, point out to your child how the mail gets delivered. Show him your mailbox, introduce him to the mail deliverer, and visit the post office. Then, use an old shoulder bag and fill it with junk mail. Sort the letters by size, putting them into paper bags or boxes. Deliver the mail to your mailbox. Go back in the house, then be yourself and go out and collect the mail. Let your child open the junk mail, look at the pictures, and throw out the opened envelopes.

....

Words of Wisdom: *My son and I challenge each other to cleaning races. We see who can get the task done faster—my dishwashing or his trains being picked up, for instance. No matter who gets done first, we both win.*

—Leanne, Westchester County, New York

170

Felt Characters

Age Range: 21 months and up

Materials

Cardboard	Scissors
Felt	Glue

Cut various oval and circular shapes out of cardboard to use as faces. Cut flesh-colored felt to fit the shape of the cardboard and glue it to the cardboard. Make all sorts of facial features: eyes, noses, mouth, mustache, glasses, hair, ears, eyebrows, or anything unusual you can think of. Use the felt board face as the base to make up characters for stories you might tell.

....

Words of Wisdom: *My daughter used to get frustrated coloring pictures with crayons because the crayon tips were so thick. I bought her colored pencils, and now she enjoys coloring much more.*

—Kathleen, Corona, California

171

Disguises

Age Range: 24 months and up

Kids love to play with disguises. Thrift stores carry a variety of cheap options: the big, soft clown nose, plastic eyeglasses with a nose attached, mustaches, and beards. Or you could try to make a few of your own.

Goggle eyes: Make crazy glasses out of pipe cleaners. The design options are endless; try spiral lenses, antennae, or embellish with cotton balls, tiny pom-poms, fringe—anything gaudy and fun. Try them on together in front of a mirror and act silly! You could even hold a photo shoot.

Paper plate masks: Make these wacky and fun—they don't have to look like anything in particular since their purpose is to disguise your face.

Veils: Take a headband and attach tulle, ribbons, and other decorations.

Animal paws: Fabric paint a footprint for an animal onto an old sock and slip it over your child's hands.

172

Masking Tape Madness

Age Range: 24 to 30 months

Masking tape is one of the most useful supplies for make-believe play. Simply by putting a piece down on the floor, you can create the boundary of a new world, the outline of a castle, many planets in the sky, weaving rivers, or paths. Make a series of intersecting roads for cars to drive on. Then pretend you are really driving the cars; honk and rev up your engine as you pass the factories and farms. Outline the floor plan of a house (the kitchen, bedroom, and backyard) so everyone knows where to place the props and where the kids need to go when the make-believe mom says it's naptime. The possibilities are endless.

173

A Rose by Any Other Color

Age Range: 24 months and up

Materials

Toilet paper tubes	Popsicle stick
Colored pieces of cellophane	Tape

Make your own rose-, blue-, green-, and yellow-colored glasses. Cut the cellophane into circles big enough to be taped over the end of a tube. Make two tubes of each color so they can be used like binoculars. Have your child look through all the different lens combinations—sometimes two of the same color, sometimes a different color in each eye— and see how the world around him changes with color.

••

Words of Wisdom: *I have my kids paint with their papers in rimmed cookie sheets—cleanup is a cinch.*

—Matt, San Diego, California

174

Voice Lessons

Age Range: 30 months and up

Toddlers are excited by all the different sounds they can make. Play with this newfound curiosity as you talk through different-sized containers, tubes, or other objects. Notice the way the sound of your voice changes a bit depending on the length and width of an object. Try using a rubber tube and letting it move around while you talk. Change the tone of your voice. See how it sounds when you stand close or far away. Try a few sound effects. Whisper, shout, giggle, and hum as you experiment with your very own noise machine. Let your child talk or hum while you softly pat his chest.

....

Words of Wisdom: *We never seem to buy doll supplies—just last week my daughter made a wonderful bed for her dolls out of a shoebox and towel.*

—Mimi, Carson City, Nevada

175

Character Spin

Age Range: 30 to 36 months

Materials
Spinning tray
Magazine pictures
Tape

Go through a magazine and find pictures of animals, people, or objects that your child could easily act out. Evenly space the pictures and tape them to the tray. Set a favorite toy on the floor next to the tray. Spin the tray around. Whatever picture stops in front of the toy will be the one your child will act out. Take turns doing the acting. Rotate the pictures once all of them have been used.

176

Finish the Story

Age Range: 36 months and up

Read a book halfway through and ask your child what she thinks might happen next. If she isn't sure how to decide, ask her what the character might do next based on what has just happened in the story. Give your child a few ideas to get her going. Then check back and see what does happen next. Or read a book almost to the end and let her finish the story with her own ending. Kids also enjoy it when a parent finishes a familiar story in a different way. That way, the child gets to tease the parent by saying, "That isn't the way it ends!"

177

Introducing Humor

Age Range: 36 months and up

Kids laugh at the silliest things. Find a way to incorporate humor into your daily lives. It may seem immature to walk into a wall or pretend to fall, but it will make your child's day. Next time you are putting your shoes on, put the sock on your hands, or put mittens on your feet. Put your clothes, jacket, and hat on backwards and then walk backwards. Pretend that the ice cubes are really hot and that sweet candy is sour. Make sure to add silly words to your sentences once in a while: "Look son, it's raining candy and ice cream!" It is never too late to act childish.

178

Nature Connection

Mud Prints

Age Range: 15 months and up

Mud provides a wonderful sensory experience. Mix the mud out in your yard by watering a patch of dirt and then stirring it with a stick. Put the mud on top of a plastic plate, then press a hand or foot firmly into the mud. Repress the urge to wiggle your fingers and toes! Decorate the print with rocks, leaves, or other natural items, then let it dry. If your child is interested in the idea of animal footprints, you may want to create a mud patch in your yard to capture the prints. Make sure to wet your mud patch down each night and then check it in the morning for visitors.

....

Words of Wisdom: *Stick a bucket outside to measure the rain or snowfall. Put a stick or ruler inside with marks for inches.*

—Kim, Park Rapids, Minnesota

179

Nature Collecting

Age Range: 15 months and up

Materials

Shoe box   Tape

Contact paper

Kids have a tendency to want to touch almost everything they see. Nature exploration offers your child an opportunity to pick up and interact with all sorts of textures and scents. Create a nature box to store little treasures on your journey into the wild. Tape contact paper sticky-side-up to the lid of the box. Things like flower pedals, leaves, grass, or other flat, lightweight objects can be attached directly to the top. The items on the top become permanent decorations for your nature box. Put bigger items inside the box.

Words of Wisdom: *Whenever we go for a walk, my daughter asks me to make a masking-tape bracelet for her. I use several widths of masking tape sticky-side-up so that my daughter can attach whatever she finds on our walk to her bracelet.*

—Tina, Grafton, Wisconsin

180

Sand Play

Age Range: 15 months and up

Sand offers unlimited tactile, building, and make-believe opportunities. Here are a few favorites:

* Take artificial flowers and "plant" a garden in your sandbox.
* Make sand saucers by filling a saucer or plate with damp sand. Press flowers or other small objects into the sand, making designs, scenes, or mandalas.
* Play a game of Find That Hand. Your child digs his hand deep into the sand as you dig your hand under from a different direction with the goal of touching fingers somewhere in the middle.
* Have a treasure hunt in the sandbox. Bury cars, blocks, small balls, and pieces of twine. Have your child use a kitchen strainer or her hands to find them.
* Build sand cities using boxes and containers on top of watered-down sand.
* Use blocks to build roads, then plant handmade flags or fences.
* Bring a plastic tea set outside and have tea parties, serving sand cookies.

181

Dry Aquarium

Age Range: 18 months and up

Materials
Large, clear plastic storage bin
Sand or colored gravel from a pet store
Plastic plants and fish

Most toddlers, when viewing a fish aquarium, would love to reach their hands into the water to feel the fish, bright plants, and plastic scenery. Since that isn't possible, why not create an aquarium your child can reach into? Fill the bottom of a storage bin with sand or colored gravel. Stick the plastic plants and decorations into the gravel. Add the plastic fish, and fill halfway up with water.

....

Words of Wisdom: *Boil seashells with bleach to clean them out so they don't smell.*
—Jason, Brecksville, Ohio

182

Feed the Birds

Age Range: 18 months and up

It's fascinating to watch birds eat. The following homemade bird feeders are sure to attract a flock.

* Roll a pine cone first in peanut butter, then in the birdseed. Hang the cone with string outside a window where it can be observed.
* Use a half-gallon cardboard milk carton. Cut out large windows on all four sides, leaving two inches at the top and bottom. Decorate the outside of the carton. Poke two holes through the top, and tie a string through each hole. Fill with birdseed.
* Cut a hole through the middle of an apple. Thread an old shoestring through and hang the apple from a tree.
* Use a needle and thread to make a string of popcorn, berries, raisins, and apples. If you have an evergreen shrub or small tree in your yard, drape the string of food around the tree.

Words of Wisdom: *Put an old baby monitor near the bird feeder so you can hear the birds.*
—Patrick, Frederick, Maryland

183

Bug Trap

Age Range: 21 months and up

Materials
Large yogurt container
Piece of cheese
4 two-inch-diameter rocks
8-inch square piece of heavy cardboard or board
Sugar cube (optional)
Magnifying glass (optional)

Dig a hole in the ground large enough to fit the yogurt container. Put a piece of cheese in the container. Place the four rocks on the dirt around the top of the yogurt container, then place the board on top, making sure the board doesn't touch the top of the yogurt container. Bugs will smell the cheese, crawl in, and not be able to get out. Check your trap each day, looking at the bugs and then letting them go. If you don't have time to set a trap, take your child outside with a sugar cube and magnifying glass. Place the cube on the ground and in a few minutes many ants will appear. Watch them through the magnifying glass.

184

Tree and Leaf Rubbings

Age Range: 21 months and up

Materials
Masking tape
Paper
Crayons

Take your tape, paper, and crayons outside. Tape the paper to a tree and gently rub the crayon across the bark using the long side, not the tip. Use different colored crayons and experiment with different tree bark to see if the design changes. Look around for interesting leaves. Put the leaves on a flat surface and tape the paper over them, then rub the crayon over the leaves. Compare the patterns of your various rubbings.

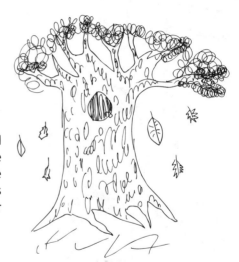

185

Egg Head

Age Range: 24 months and up

Materials
Cress seeds
Cotton balls
Eggshells
Old egg carton
Felt markers

Using half an eggshell, draw a face with markers, and then set the shell in the egg carton. Soak cotton balls in water and place them inside the eggshell. Sprinkle cress seeds on top of the cotton balls. Set the carton in a window sill for a few days, making sure to keep the cotton moist. Soon, "hair" will be growing out of the eggshell!

186

Nature Museum Display

Age Range: 24 months and up

Materials
Large matchboxes
Sheet of cotton
Piece of cardboard large enough
to glue all the boxes onto

Glue matchboxes onto the cardboard. Put cotton in the bottom of each box. Decide together what you want to display: rocks, seashells, leaves, bark, feathers, or whatever you like. Then go on a walk to begin gathering for your museum. You may not be able to find everything on one walk, since this is a collection that may take time to complete. Display it someplace where everyone in the family can see it. Your child will be proud to play show-and-tell with what has been found!

187

Magnify It

Age Range: 24 months and up

Toddlers love to see things up close. Gather a variety of interesting items in a basket or box, then sit together on a blanket outside and get a close-up view. Hold a magnifying glass up to each item. Let your child look at and then describe what he sees. Help him to use descriptive words like "rough," "smooth," "dark," "light," "thin," "thick," "hard," and "soft." Pick two or three favorite items and then go on a hunt to find them in the wild. Take your magnifying glass along so you can observe them close-up in their natural environment.

Words of Wisdom: *I keep an oversized umbrella in the car year-round—it's great for propping in the sandbox or on the beach on hot days.*
—Amy, New Ulm, Minnesota

188

Blossoming Bulbs

Age Range: 30 to 36 months

Buy narcissus, daffodils, amaryllis, crocus, tulips, or other bulbs (ask your local nursery for recommendations). The bulbs don't even need soil. Just "plant" them in enough water to cover the lower portion of the bulb, but don't submerse them. You can use a vase for this purpose, or support the bulb in almost any glass container. Surround it with rocks, marbles, or beads, and add water to halfway up the bulb. Set it in a warm, bright spot, and water regularly. Watch stalks sprout and roots snake down looking for water. Have a calendar nearby to cross off the days until the bulb blooms, which should take about a month. Move the bulb out of the sun and into a cooler spot when the blooms begin to appear so they'll last as long as possible.

189

Wind Sock

Age Range: 30 to 36 months

Remove the lid and cut off the bottom of a cylindrical cardboard oatmeal box. Cover the box with construction or contact paper, and have your child decorate it with paint, markers, or glued bunches of paper. Together glue, tape, or staple crepe paper streamers to the inside of one end of the box. Punch four holes in the other end (across from one another). Tie one string, about twelve inches long, to two opposing holes, and another to the other two holes. Gather them both with a third, longer piece of string, which you will use to hang the wind sock. If possible, hang it outside a prominent window in the house so your child will see it often. Use it to take a wind prediction or measurement each day.

190

Moon Watch

Age Range: 36 months and up

Materials
Black construction paper
White chalk or paint

Go outside one night per week for a month and look at the moon. Help your child to draw or paint the shape you see. Point out how the moon's shape changes each week. Looking at the sky at night creates a peaceful feeling, so enjoy these moments together. Young children often wonder why the moon follows them. Try answering that question!

Words of Wisdom: *My youngest child's favorite thing to do in the dark at night is to pretend to blow out the flashlight. He blows it just like a candle, and as he blows, I turn off the light.*
—Stacey, Studio City, California

191

Snail Farm

Age Range: 36 months and up

Materials
Clear plastic bottle
Bean bag or play dough
Soil
Lettuce or weeds
Snails from the garden

Your snail farm will be contained within the plastic bottle. Cut a small door in the side of the bottle about three inches by two inches so that when the bottle is on its side, the door is at the top. Next, place damp soil in the bottle. Go outside and look for snails in the yard, around leafy plants, in the vegetable garden, or at the base of brick walls. Put them in your snail farm and give them fresh food like lettuce and weeds. Seal the door at the top with some clear tape, and punch holes in the tape for air vents. Make sure the bottle top is on. Watch your snails for a few days, then let them go.

192

Floor Time
Adventures

Bicycling

Age Range: 15 months and up

Have your child lie on her back. Hold her feet or ankles and help her bicycle her legs rhythmically while you sing, "Bicycle, bicycle riding along… Bicycle, bicycle all the day long…Bicycle, bicycle isn't it fun…On your bicycle, bicycle out in the sun." When she's coordinated enough, switch places and let her bicycle your legs.

Words of Wisdom: *Take turns laying your head on one another's belly and talking or singing. The next time you're laughing, put your child's ear to your stomach. Giggling is highly contagious.*

—Audry, Wyomissing, Pennsylvania

193

Partner Exercises

Age Range: 15 months and up

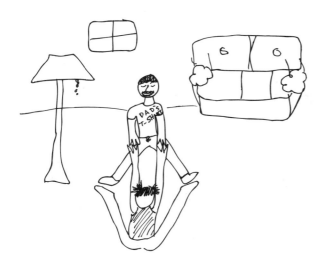

Boating: Sit across from each other on the floor with the soles of your feet touching. Hold hands and rock back and forth. When the adult leans forward, the child leans back, and vice versa. Sing "Row, Row, Row Your Boat" as you imagine rowing along in the river.

Popping: Sit with your legs stretched out in front of you and your child on your legs facing you. Hold hands. Sing "Pop Goes the Weasel," bouncing your legs to the tune, and slide your legs apart at the "pop!" so the toddler falls down. Really build up the suspense by going slowly, then quickly.

194

Planting Garden Massage

Age Range: 18 months and up

Kneel alongside your child, who is face down on the floor. Begin with a back-and-forth scissors motion with flat hands starting at the bottom of the back and moving upward. Think of this as the tractor turning the soil. Then gently swoop to the bottom with the outside of one of your hands forming a C-shape. Keep the other hand comfortably but firmly on the lower back. Swoop in the middle, on the right, and on the left…you're smoothing the soil. Then begin making holes to plant the seeds—make small circles all over the back with the pads of your fingers, but don't poke! Take this opportunity to engage your child—ask what kinds of seeds she's planting. Then comb down the back with the pads of your fingers, gently raking the soil over the freshly planted seeds. There's nothing like a little rain to water the seedlings—gently pitter patter your fingers all over her back. Then enjoy a gentle wind blowing away any clouds—here you don't actually touch your child. Blow soft breaths from her head to toes.

195

Jar Play

Age Range: 21 to 24 months

Toddlers enjoy the feeling of doing simple actions by themselves. Buy a bunch of large plastic jars with screw-on tops. Put toys, household items, or other found objects in each of the jars, making sure to close the top. Give the jars to your child and encourage him to get the items out. Let him figure out for himself how the jars open. Once he gets them open, allow him to fill them with other things, close them and try to open them again. These kind of jars make great permanent storage containers.

196

Magic-Carpet Rides

Age Range: 21 months and up

Lay your child on top of a blanket or beach towel on the floor. Tell him to hold on to the edges as he wraps them around himself. Then pull slowly across a smoothly surfaced floor and magically transport yourself to different locations on your magic-carpet ride. Call the magic carpet a boat and pretend that water is all around. Dip your oars into the water; say, "Aye aye, Captain"; and look out for sharks as you decide where to go. Then make it a spaceship and head off for Planet Ice Cream or some other magical place.

197

Antigravity Machine

Age Range: 24 months and up

Hold your child securely by the waist so she can bounce around like an astronaut. Support her as she walks up the walls and across the ceiling. Head outside and let her walk up trees and fences. This is a workout for the adult holding the little astronaut, so you may want to put a time limit on this game. It is also fun to watch a video or read a book about astronauts in space before beginning so your child can expand this exercise and her imagination.

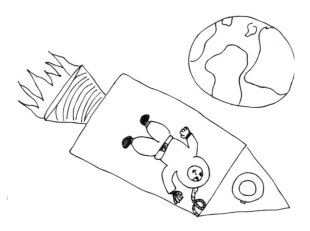

198

Obstacle Course

Age Range: 24 months and up

Use pillows, blankets, couch cushions, chairs, or anything else you find around the house to create an obstacle course. Tape masking tape in a line on the floor leading from one part of the course to the other. Perhaps it begins in the kitchen where your child needs to put a bunch of boxes into a laundry basket, then proceeds down the hall where she touches a circle on the wall—whatever you want to create. Then try marching through the course or going through the course to music.

....

Words of Wisdom: *Have your child do exercise videos with you. This makes it more fun for you, and you also don't feel as conspicuous!*
—Amy, Savannah, Georgia

199

Parachutes

Age Range: 24 months and up

Materials
Cloth napkin or handkerchief
String or ribbon
Paper clip or small toy

Attach a twelve-inch long piece of string or ribbon to each corner of the piece of cloth. Bring the string together and tie a knot at about the nine-inch mark. Attach a paper clip or light plastic toy figure to the string. You may have to experiment with the weight of the attached figure and the size of the cloth to make sure the parachute drifts slowly to the ground instead of falling too quickly and landing with a bang. Wad the parachute up and toss it into the air, or drop it from above. Watch the excitement on your child's face as it floats to the ground.

200

Seesaw

Age Range: 24 months and up

Materials
Book
Paper tube
Newspaper
Small toys or stuffed animals

Take the tube and stuff it full of newspaper. Lay the tube horizontally on the floor. Put the book on top of the tube, balanced in the middle like a seesaw. Collect a basket of small toys and stuffed animals and put one at a time on the down side of the seesaw. Push the up side of the seesaw down, and watch the toy fly in the air. After all animals have had a chance to fly, pick them up and start again.

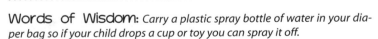

Words of Wisdom: *Carry a plastic spray bottle of water in your diaper bag so if your child drops a cup or toy you can spray it off.*
—David E., Houston, Texas

201

Follow That Noise

Age Range: 30 months and up

Teach your child how to follow a noise by hiding a musical wind-up toy in a room somewhere in the house. Help her learn to find it before the music runs out, or you might use a portable radio so there is no time crunch. Later you might try to hide somewhere in the house and see if your child can find you. You will need to make lots of noise so she can follow the sound.

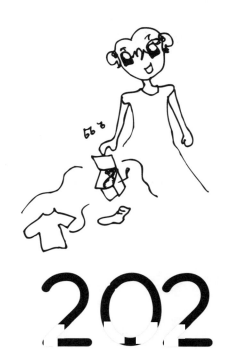

. . . .

Words of Wisdom: *My son's favorite game is to have me hide somewhere in the house and make pig sounds. He thinks they sound so funny, so the whole time he's looking for me he laughs. So, of course, I start laughing and he finds me right away.*

—Ginger, Huntington Beach, California

202

Mini-Golf

Age Range: 30 to 36 months

Materials
Wrapping-paper tube
Toilet-paper tube
Aluminum foil
Containers, boxes, or cans

Make a golf club out of a wrapping-paper tube taped to a toilet-paper tube. Cut a slot at the bottom of the wrapping-paper tube about two inches long and insert the end of a flattened toilet paper tube into it. Make a ball out of rolled up aluminum foil. You can use almost anything for the holes on your golf course: containers, boxes, or cans. If it's a warm day, go outside to play golf, and if your yard allows, make some real holes in the ground.

203

Sound Walk

Age Range: 30 months and up

Gather a variety of drumsticks—metal spoons, wooden spoons, chopsticks, unsharpened pencils with eraser ends, or a small baby sock stuffed with cotton balls and securely fastened to the end of a wooden dowel. Take a walk around the house and try them out gently on different surfaces—on the floor, the wall, your legs, your belly, the chair, the table, the couch, a window, a hollow box, or a can. Try copying any rhythm your child taps out, and then see if she can copy a simple rhythm of yours.

204

Wheel Hunting

Age Range: 30 months and up

While singing the song "The Wheels on the Bus Go Round and Round," pretend to drive each other around the house looking for wheels—anything round you find among your furnishings, toys, food, dishes, and closets should be tested. Try out the way the wheels or circular objects work by pushing a truck or car across the floor or sticking a pencil through a loose toy tire to watch it spin in a circle. Roll a plastic cup on its side, or spin a circular tray. Go outside for a walk and look for circular objects or wheels in the world around you.

205

Around the House

Toy Spinner

Age Range: 15 months and up

Next time you're preparing a meal, organizing a drawer, making phone calls, or cleaning, create some spinning entertainment for your child. Put a lazy Susan or some kind of spinning tray on the floor. Place various small toys or nonbreakable household objects on the tray. Spin the tray and see what happens. Does the object fly off or stay put as it goes around and around? Is there a difference if the object is placed close to the center versus near the edge? If your child likes to watch the object spinning around without falling off, you may want to tape it to the tray with masking tape.

206

Cabinet Play

Age Range: 15 months and up

Cabinets are tempting, especially in the kitchen where they are at eye level for your child. Clear out one lower cabinet and fill it with unbreakable kitchen tools your toddler is allowed to play with. To surprise your child with new items, hide toys or other interesting objects in cookie tins. Change or rotate the items in the cabinet regularly to keep it interesting. If you are making a special dish for dinner, put some of the needed equipment in her cabinet so she can help organize the meal.

• •

Words of Wisdom: *My daughter's favorite kitchen activity is to sort the silverware for me. Of course, I take any sharp objects out first. Then I put the silverware basket and silverware tray on the kitchen table and let her put them away.*

—May, St. Paul, Minnesota

207

Put In, Take Out

Age Range: 15 months and up

Materials
Empty boxes with dividers
Paper tubes, plastic bottles, toys

Next time you're out grocery shopping, stop by the liquor department of the store and ask for a few boxes that have the bottle dividers still in them. When you are home unloading the groceries, give your child a bunch of paper tubes, toys, or plastic bottles for him to put into the box. If you have more than one box, your child can pretend to be packing the boxes for shipping, or he might enjoy moving the items from one box to the other. Putting objects into things and then taking them out again is fun for toddlers.

● ●

Words of Wisdom: *My daughter is always entertained playing with magnets I've put on the bottom half of the refrigerator. I get so much of my kitchen work done while she's perfectly happy entertaining herself.*

—Cathy, Bloomington, Minnesota

208

Sock Duster Games

Age Range: 24 months and up

Little hands make good dusters. Save your mismatched socks and keep them in the cleaning box. Have your child put a sock on each hand and get ready to play the following dusting games:

❋ Decide where you are going to dust; then draw a line down the middle and have a race to see which one of you gets your side dusted first.

❋ Let your child spray a design on the furniture with dusting spray, then erase the design as he dusts the table.

❋ Let your child do the time-consuming dusting of small, nonbreakable objects. Ask him to lift the item off the shelf with socks on his hands and then rub his hands all over the dusty object before putting it back on the shelf.

Words of Wisdom: *I give my son a soft, thick-bristled paintbrush to help me when I dust.*

—Barb, Ventura, California

209

Oops! Day

Age Range: 18 months and up

Kids love everything goofy and unexpected, so make a point today to make them laugh at the silly things you do. Make a big production of putting your shoes on your hands instead of your feet, putting your coat on backwards, looking for milk in the silverware drawer, calling the cat by the wrong name. Then give an exaggerated, "Ooooops!" and watch your child howl with laughter. Let him "catch" you fouling things up before you "notice" your mistake, and he'll laugh even harder!

....

Words of Wisdom: *I buy my toilet paper wrapped as individual roles so my daughter can stack it like blocks. They are light, stack easily, and are still wrapped up when we need to use them.*

—John, Apple Valley, Minnesota

210

Place Mats

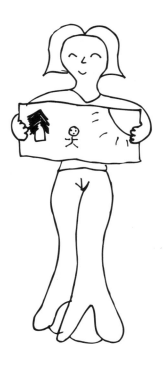

Age Range: 18 months and up

Toddlers love to see their artwork turned into place mats for the whole family to enjoy and admire. Place mat construction can be as easy as taking a painting or drawing to be laminated or covering it with contact paper. Try decorating a piece of colored paper with a bunch of shapes, or create a scene from a coloring book. It's also fun to make up a place mat showing the proper placement of plate, silverware, napkin, and cup so she can practice. Go to the library and make copies of pictures of the birds or animals you might find in your area. Glue them onto construction paper and include the bird's name so your child can point out the birds at the feeder while she eats breakfast.

211

Grocery Shopping

Age Range: 21 months and up

Make a habit of saving empty food boxes, yogurt containers, plastic ketchup bottles, or other packaging that your child might be interested in shopping for at his make-believe home grocery store. Make sure to tape or secure any paper labels that are peeling, glue the lids or tops on, and store them in a cardboard box. On grocery day, take the box out and place the items around the house. Let your child use a grocery bag or a toy grocery cart to do her shopping. Once she fills her bag or cart, help her to put the groceries away in the make-believe kitchen.

Words of Wisdom: *There are lots of games to play while grocery shopping. My son's favorite is to call out the name of the food or the food group of each grocery item as I put it in the basket.*

—Jen, Omaha, Nebraska

212

Bath Book

Age Range: 21 months and up

Take a sequence of bathtime photos: shots with bubbles all around, fish-lip faces, and funny wet hairdos. Gather several Ziploc baggies and cut construction paper pieces to fit into them. Then help your child select which bathtime photos she'd like to glue onto the construction paper—both front and back. Then help her seal them inside the bags and order them however she likes (maybe have her make a personalized cover page). Sew the bags together outside the zipper part (so the pages will remain sealed and waterproof) with needle and thread or with a hole punch and yarn.

Words of Wisdom: *Try using a turkey baster to rinse your child's hair in the bath. My son is now tearless when I wash his hair since no soap gets in his eyes.*

—Deborah, Orient, Ohio

213

Getting It Done

Age Range: 24 months and up

Take note of the places where you spend daily chunks of time, like the bedroom getting ready, the home office working on the computer, the garage puttering, or the kitchen cooking. Make sure there is a stool, bench, or chair available for your child at each location so he always feels welcome to sit and chat while you're accomplishing something. The goal is to communicate interactively, involving and teaching your child about what you are doing. Here's his chance to be a mini-you—give him an old checkbook when you are paying the bills or part of the newspaper while you are reading it. You'll be amazed at all the daily tasks you can accomplish when you know you're both working *and* spending time with your child.

214

Reading Nook

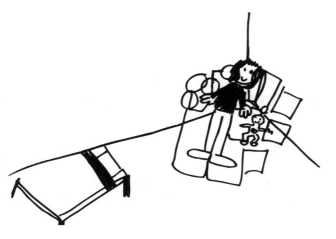

Age Range: 24 months and up

Create a reading nook somewhere in the house—a place that's quiet, cozy, and well lit, with lots of cushions and a blanket. Rotate a basket of books so that there are always fresh ones, or perhaps this can be the place you keep borrowed library books. Make a point of spending daily time in the nook sharing books with your child.

....

Words of Wisdom: *I pretend that I'm going to "eat" toys with the vacuum unless they're in the right place. The kids scramble to pick everything up out of my path, giggling the whole time.*
—Heather, Washington, Utah

215

Help Wanted

Age Range: 24 months and up

Toddlers love to be of help. Get your child involved in simple chores, like feeding the cat, setting the table, holding the dust pan, using a push vacuum, wiping out the bathroom sink, helping collect laundry, lining up shoes, or matching socks. Decorate a coffee jar or shoebox and write "Help Wanted" on it. Write the jobs on slips of paper or, for younger children, draw pictures of the activity. Whenever your child seems bored or wants to do exactly what you are doing, let her pick a job from the jar. Believe it or not, with practice she'll soon be more of a help than a hindrance! Give lots of positive reinforcement for whatever effort is made.

● ●

Words of Wisdom: *When our son had been walking for a year, we decided to install a handrail on our stairway about ten inches below the handrail the adults use. He now walks up and down the stairs safely with great confidence.*
—Mike, Seattle, Washington

216

Tent Fun

Age Range: 30 to 36 months

Here's a way to make laundry day fun for your toddler. Take all the dirty sheets off the beds and let your toddler play with them. He can make a fort, tent, stage curtain, cape, magic carpet, river, or whatever he can imagine. When your child tires of playing with the sheets, wash them and put them back on the beds together.

••

Words of Wisdom: *My daughter wanted to climb the stairs so badly. To make it safe, I put the baby gate three steps off the bottom of the staircase so she could practice and have fun climbing without getting hurt.*

—Mary Jane, Boston, Massachusetts

217

Window Art

Age Range: 30 months and up

Large outdoor windows make an ideal painting surface for poster or finger paint and can be easily sprayed clean when the artist has finished enjoying his work. Make it a family tradition to paint the outside windows before you do the spring window cleaning. Let your child create a design on the patio doors or other reachable window space. This is also fun to do for various holidays: paint a ghost or pumpkins at Halloween or a snowman in the winter. Once the paint is dry, it will stay on the window until washed off with soap and water.

....

Words of Wisdom: *Every time I have to clean the bathroom, I give my daughter a new box of Kleenex. She absolutely loves pulling them out one at a time. I then use those tissues to stick in my purse, in the car, or in our travel bag.*

—Margi, Salt Lake City, Utah

218

How Does Your Garden Grow?

Age Range: 30 months and up

Help your toddler learn to nurture life and appreciate nature through the tending of a garden. Together, select plants from local nurseries and seed catalogs, plant them, water them, weed them, and watch them grow. Kids love digging in wet earth, playing with earthworms, and pouring water from a watering can. Plant a row of fast-growing sunflowers for immediate success. It's a messy endeavor, so wear garden clothes! Plus, if you try a vegetable garden (cherry tomatoes, carrots, and potatoes are all very satisfying for child gardeners), you'll have the added benefit of getting her to eat more vegetables! Avoid pesticides or sharp gardening tools.

219

Section Three:
Out and About

Traveling with Toddlers

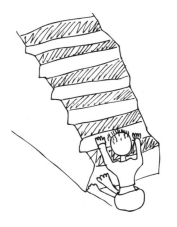
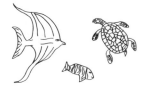

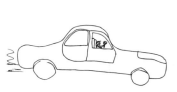

Count Together

Age Range: 15 months and up

Kids love to count everything and will soon get used to counting from one to ten if you do it often enough. You can count stairs, bites of cereal, pillows on the couch, cars on the road, chairs at a table, trees on a hike, waves at the ocean, or rocks on the walkway. Wherever you are, make counting a part of your life. Sing, clap, or make up rhymes as you practice your numbers.

• •

Words of Wisdom: *We are friends with another couple with young children. Occasionally we travel together—short, inexpensive, nearby get-aways that are fun for the whole family. We go for at least two nights each time so we can swap child-sitting services. Then each couple can get a special, kid-free evening knowing the kids are safe and happy with familiar friends.*

—Bill, Oak Park, Illinois

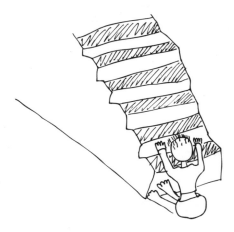

220

Activity Bag

Age Range: 15 months and up

Whenever you travel, take some time to create an activity bag filled with things your child likes to play with: favorite books, dolls, pipe cleaners, finger puppets, and other quiet, non-messy toys. These will entertain your child and give him something to do while in hotel rooms, on a plane, or in any other space where he doesn't have his usual supply of toys. A backpack makes a good activity bag. Your child can carry it himself, and it has lots of extra compartments where you can also pack snacks.

Words of Wisdom: *Always carry crayons (save the ones you get in the little packs at restaurants) and a pad of paper as well as a few of the teeny sponges that grow in a glass of water (available at children's or art and craft stores). They'll get you through restaurant waits.*

—Vickie, Williston, North Dakota

221

Toddler-Proofing Kit

Age Range: 15 months and up

Too often, parents set out to have a fun vacation only to find they spend most of their time following their toddler around Grandma's house or the rented vacation home, making sure their child is safe. Make a toddler-proofing kit and keep it in your car so you'll be prepared no matter where you stay. The kit should include electric socket protectors, a toilet lock, rubber bands for kitchen cabinets, masking tape for cords, and corner guards. As soon as you arrive, take ten minutes to survey your location. Put the rubber bands on the kitchen cabinets, look for any loose cords and tape them out of the way, and shut all bathroom doors. If your toddler is at the door-slamming stage, put a towel over the top of all the doors. Secure the socket-protectors and toilet lock, and then enjoy your time away from home.

222

Games to Play in a Restaurant

Age Range: 18 months and up

- Outline objects like keys, lipstick, table glasses, or a fork on the back of your place mat.
- Make rubbings of coins, credit cards, or any other flat object on your table. Peel the paper off of the crayon. Put the object on the table, place paper on top, and rub over it with a crayon.
- Play the money fountain game. Fill your glass almost to the top with water. Give each person a few coins. Go around the table and let each person drop a coin into the water. The person whose coin makes the water overflow loses.
- Show your child a small object. Have him shut his eyes while you hide it someplace on the table—possibly under a napkin or glass or beneath an overturned spoon.

223

Games to Play in the Car

Age Range: 18 months and up

* Bring along puppets or stuffed animals to represent the characters in one of your audio stories. Play the story and encourage your toddler to use the puppets to act out the story as it is being played.
* Keep a kitchen timer in the car at all times. This is great for guessing how long it will be before you see a certain object, how long until you get to stop, or how much longer until you arrive at your destination.
* Bring a role of scotch tape. Give kids pieces of paper, bags, cups, or other trash items (you can ask for extras at the fast-food window so that the paper isn't sticky), and let them make a trip sculpture.
* Make an edible necklace. Use Cheerios or Fruit Loops and thin shoelaces with plastic tips. String the cereal onto the shoestring and tie both ends together to make a necklace.
* Laminate a drawing or painting of roads and parking lots that fits snugly into a cookie sheet or jelly-roll pan with sides. Tape the picture into the cookie sheet, or paint it directly onto a cookie sheet you can sacrifice and keep in the car. Let your child run small cars over it when you are driving.

224

Games to Play on a Plane

Age Range: 18 months and up

- Make a puppet out of an airsick bag. Use two or more, and you'll be able to create a story to act out.
- Use the headphones and pretend to talk through the end of the cord into each other's ears, or pretend to be pilots flying the plane and listening through the headphones for directions from ground control.
- Rip pictures out of the flight magazine and make up a story with them, or ask each other questions about items in the pictures.
- Sort the snack packets into piles and count them.
- Make up a clapping rhythm to match each person who walks down the aisle past your seat.
- Play "What Is Missing?" by putting six items on the tray. Have your child close his eyes and then take one item away. He gets to guess which item you took away. Take turns.
- When all else fails, dig into your purse and pull out a compact mirror—a guaranteed half-hour of entertainment. (You may want to buy these especially for play so that your makeup isn't ruined!)

225

Games to Play while Standing in Line

Age Range: 24 months and up

- I Spy: Look for an object in your immediate surroundings and give your child clues as to what you're looking at, by saying something like "I spy with my little eye something that is red."
- Draw faces on your fingers or thumbs with a pen, and then act out a story.
- Play a counting game with the people ahead of you in line. Count how many there are, or how many men or women, people with red hair or black hair, people with glasses, or anything else you can think to count.
- If you're outside, take a look up at the sky and ask your child what shapes she sees in the clouds. Then make up a story about the shapes.

226

Words of Wisdom: *Since my son was a baby, I've taken him with me to vote. It's a learning experience that has been fun for him, plus he loves the "I voted" stickers. Any place you go can be fun for a toddler if you allow extra time to discuss what's happening.*

—Robin, Little Rock, Arkansas

What Do They Have in Common?

Age Range: 24 months and up

Ask what do_____ and_____ have in common? Allow your child to think about the question and figure out a common characteristic. What do grass and a tree have in common? They are both green. What do a fish and a dolphin have in common? They both live in the water or both have a fin. Whatever your child thinks of and offers as an answer, try to elaborate on and stretch to make the answer correct.

••

Words of Wisdom: *On my first business trip after becoming a parent, I found myself watching other parents with their children in airports. They were so rushed and stressed that they forgot to explain what to expect from things like security checks, metal detectors, and moving walkways. No wonder kids act out! I vowed to remember that what is mundane to me is new— and sometimes overwhelming and even scary—to my kids and to take the time to make traveling better for all of us.*

—Julianne, Greensboro, North Carolina

227

Coloring on the Go

Age Range: 24 months and up

Make photocopies of pages from coloring books. You can find tons of printable ones online or make your own on the computer. Have them laminated at the copy shop. If you make half-sized sheets the paper goes further and it fits better in your bag. Then punch holes through them and bind a bunch together with round binder clips, creating a personalized dry-erase/sticker book. Also include a binder pencil case, which you can use to hold the dry-erase markers and removable stickers. For older toddlers include some games—matching colors, missing pieces, and so forth. Look to store-bought activity books for ideas—but make them your own by personalizing them.

228

Postcards Home

Age Range: 24 months and up

Create a permanent reminder of all the places you visited on your trip. Buy a postcard at each location—even gas stations and motels along the way can become prime locations and memories for a child. When you end your travels for the day, take some time to write what you did, saw, bought, or liked about that location. Ask your toddler to help you remember! Then send the postcard home. Your toddler will be surprised and excited as each postcard arrives in the mailbox. Enjoy recognizing, remembering, and talking about the familiar locations you visited together on your trip.

Words of Wisdom: *I sometimes double- and triple-wrap the toys and food treats I keep in my purse—the entertainment value lasts longer that way.*
—Sandy, Kailua-Kona, Hawaii

229

Cheap Thrills

Age Range: 24 months and up

The everyday things that go on in the world are incredibly interesting to toddlers. Take your child with you to a car wash where you're allowed to sit inside the car. Make sure you park your car first and watch another car going through so the loud noises or spinning mops won't scare him. Then go and visit a Laundromat with all the spinning washers and dryers going round and round. Take a bus to the park instead of driving. These are inexpensive, everyday adventures that your toddler will talk about for months to come. Make sure to take photos.

••

Words of Wisdom: *If you have one of those child-sized play shopping carts at home, take it along on errands with you and not just to the grocery store! They will keep the kids amused for ages. Remember to have them put their own snack and drink bottle in there. They'll enjoy being responsible for their own things.*

—Val, Meridian, Mississippi

230

Guess What Game

Age Range: 30 months and up

Describe something you see inside a restaurant, outside a car window, while you're walking through a mall, or wherever you are with your child. Give three clues to your child, saying, "The first clue is_____." Then give him a few moments to think about that clue and get a few ideas. Then give the second clue, saying, "The second clue is _____." Finish with the third clue. Your toddler will feel proud when he guesses the answer. Through this fun game, your toddler is counting, making inferences, and organizing information—all early thinking skills and simple problem-solving that will make him more aware of his environment.

231

Travel Stationery

Age Range: 30 to 36 months

Make sure to bring the addresses of family and friends on your next vacation. Pack a Ziploc bag full of stickers so that kids can turn ordinary hotel stationery or blank paper into personalized stationery. Encourage kids to tell you what they remember about the day so you can write it down for them. This is a great way to help kids remember what they did that day while at the same time sharing all the vacation news with family and friends. Your child can sign the letter with a personalized scribble or picture.

232

Backseat Drivers

Age Range: 30 to 36 months

Before you leave on your trip, cut a large red circle and a large green circle out of construction paper. Glue them each to a Popsicle stick. Write "stop" on one and "go" on the other. Whenever you stop the car, ask your toddler to hold up the red circle. When the car begins to move, have him hold up the green circle. This is fun while going through a city, rush hour traffic, or anywhere there are many stops and goes. It also teaches the concept of stop and go. If your child doesn't like the idea of holding sticks in his hands, simply ask him to say "stop" when he sees a red light and "go" when he sees a green light.

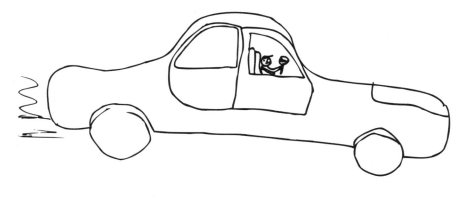

233

Friends and Playgroups

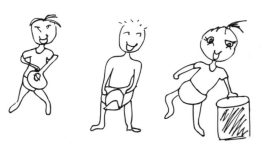

Why Start a Playgroup?

Age Range: 15 months and up

* It's a welcome diversion from everyday routine and a chance to focus on nothing but having fun with your child without distraction from phone calls, email, work deadlines, chores, or errands.
* If your child isn't in daycare or preschool, playgroup will offer him the chance to meet playmates his own age and become comfortable interacting with other adults.
* If your child is in daycare or preschool, it's a great way for him to get some dedicated time to play with you. If your little one has older siblings, playgroup will give her much-needed one-on-one time with you and the companionship of other kids who don't see her as "the baby" of the bunch.
* Bonding with other parents is important. Playgroups are not just for stay-at-home parents—many are offered on evenings or weekends—and they aren't just for moms either. Look for playgroups offered through mother or father clubs, parenting associations, Baby and Me classes, or book clubs. Venture online for around-the-clock, across-the-globe support!
* The playgroup is useful for establishing a baby-sitting co-op so you can go out while your child plays with friends.

Setting up a Playgroup

Age Range: 15 months and up

* Schedule a meeting with only the adults to iron out the logistics like schedule, location, and duties of the host. Make sure to rotate locations.
* Keep playgroups as simple as possible by inviting no more than six children. Make sure the kids are no more than six months apart in age so that games and activities are appropriate for all.
* The host should supply no more than simple snacks. This is not a home show or gourmet-cooking competition.
* Surround yourself with people who are supportive, warm, and friendly, and whose parenting styles are compatible with or complementary to your own. Remember, these fellow parents serve as role models for your child, as you do for theirs.
* You're not expected to totally childproof your home to host a playgroup, but do alert the other parents to potential dangers and try to make the designated play area as safe as possible. If you have a dog that is likely to scare the little ones or a cat that's skittish around children, lock the pet up.
* Watch your child closely; other parents don't want to be in the awkward position of trying to discipline your child.
* The golden rule: no sick children allowed under any circumstance.

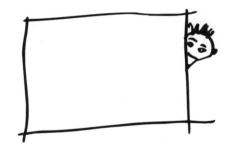

235

Bag of Tricks

Age Range: 15 months and up

Keep these few playgroup essentials up your sleeve:

First-aid kit: It's Murphy's Law—if you have it, you won't need it. Make sure to stock the basics—Band-Aids, antibiotic cream, butterfly bandages, gauze pads, and white tape.

Kid-friendly music: Find a few kids' music CDs that are funny and action-oriented. Some songs even come with directions for things the kids can do while singing. Parents can do the actions with the words so the kids know what to do.

Car kit essentials: Sunscreen, tarp or blanket (no more wet bottoms from a freshly watered lawn!), bubbles, sidewalk chalk (wrap one end in masking tape—no more stained fingers!), sand toys (buckets, shovels, cookie cutters, Jell-O molds, funnels, and containers), and sanitizing gel.

Calling cards: Create a family business card to hand out if you meet someone at a park with whom you'd like to get together for a playdate. Include your name, child's name, telephone number, and address.

236

Parade Time

Age Range: 15 months and up

Have a parade. Each child can hold a stuffed animal or favorite toy and march around to music. Scarves are also fun to wave overhead. Adults can also participate by stepping into the parade or bringing up the rear, encouraging little stragglers. Change leaders every few minutes so everyone has a chance to direct the group. If the kids are old enough, the leader can do actions, like jumping, twirling, or kicking his legs up. You can also create a musical parade by asking each child to bring an instrument or give everyone a pot or lid to bang. Or meet at a park and have a rolling parade with tricycles, bikes, or strollers. Bring flags and streamers and make a spectacle of yourselves!

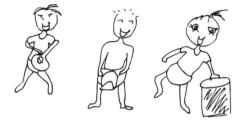

Words of Wisdom: *We keep a dry-erase board just inside the pantry door. On it we have both kids' names and a list of foods that they are currently eating without issue. It makes life easier for caretakers who might try to give our son cheese slices when all he will eat is shredded cheese.*

—Sonya, Menlo Park, California

237

Beanbag Group Games

Age Range: 15 months and up

Materials
Beanbags
Hula hoop, laundry basket, buckets

There are so many things you can do with beanbags. Here are a few to try with a group:

Bucket catch: Someone throws a beanbag and a child tries to catch it in a bucket she is holding.

Crawl race: Put a beanbag on each child's back and have them crawl around the room. Each time a beanbag falls off, someone puts it back on and the race continues.

Hula ring: Put the hula hoop down on the floor and try to throw the beanbags into the center. Begin by standing close to it, then move farther and farther away as skill increases.

Pass the bag: Sit in a circle with music playing. When the music is slow, pass the beanbag slowly; when the music is fast, pass faster; and when the music stops, someone is left holding the bag. That child stands up and does a quick dance.

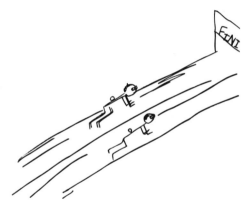

238

Toddler Safari

Age Range: 18 months and up

Invite playgroup members to bring a couple of stuffed animals each. Put the animals in a laundry basket when the kids arrive. Have the kids do a welcome song or activity while a few of the parents hide the animals (not *too* well!) around the room or backyard. Before going on safari to find all the animals, have each child make a set of binoculars out of empty toilet-paper rolls. Tape the rolls together with masking tape. Use a hole punch on either side and add a length of yarn for a strap. Then go hunting in the jungle for animals! Once all the animals are sighted, you can hide them and begin again. It is also fun to have the kids act like each animal as soon as they spot it. Serve animal crackers as a snack.

Words of Wisdom: *Since we rotate houses for playgroup, the host picks up the toys afterwards (when the children are too young to really help). That way, parents only pick up toys at their own house where they know where they belong—and the other parents get the morning off.*

—Leigh Ann, York, Nebraska

239

Presto Pizza

Age Range: 21 months and up

Create a pizza parlor. Gather felt of several colors (tan for the crust, red for the sauce, yellow for the cheese, black for the olives, green for the bell peppers, pink for pepperoni). Cut the tan felt into extra-large-sized pizza crusts. Then cut out the colored felt to use as ingredients to put on top of the crust. Give each group of two or three kids one crust and have them work to make a pizza by decorating it with the other pieces of felt. Serve pizza as a snack.

240

Group Dance Games

Age Range: 21 months and up

Freeze dance: Most children are wonderful dancers—they wiggle, turn, jump, and move to music. Turn on some music and tell the children to dance until the music stops. When the music stops, everyone freezes. They can march around, crawl around, or whatever they like, but whenever the music stops, they stop.

Touch dance: Have the kids stand in a circle. Tap one child on the shoulder to begin the dance while everyone watches. When finished the dancer touches the child next to him, and that child takes a turn in the spotlight. The dances can be very short or up to thirty seconds. They can be fast, slow, up high, or down low. Encourage the kids to keep the dance moving around the circle.

241

Sharing

Age Range: 21 months and up

It is not easy for kids this age to share a toy. It's totally age-appropriate for children under three years to play alongside one another, each with their own toy rather than with one another. Here are some sharing ground rules:

* Playdate toys are for sharing, whether at home or out and about. Put away or keep at home your child's favorite toys if she isn't prepared to let others play with them.
* Expect toy-yanking and lots of "Mine!" struggles, regardless—toddlers are very possessive.
* Help them to negotiate with one another (trading toys, offering one coveted toy for another), and encourage them to be gentle.
* Think of games and activities that include the whole group in a physical activity or individual art or craft project. If toys are to be the focus, make sure each child brings her own.

242

Field Trips

Age Range: 24 months and up

Local bakery: Most toddlers are amazed to watch a donut being stamped from a mold, a wedding cake decorated, or cookies made. It is especially fun when they get to taste the results. Call local bakeries to see if any offer tours.

Pizza restaurant: Many pizza chain restaurants offer schools and play-groups a special tour during morning hours when pizza production is slow. Sometimes they even let the kids shape the dough and make their own pizzas.

Farm: Depending on the make-up of your neighborhood you may have a dairy farm, orchard, or crop-producing facility in your immediate area. Find out what time of day or year is the best time to watch the farmer in action. Read about the kind of farm you'll be seeing so that the kids are prepared.

Fire station: Most fire departments look forward to a visit from toddlers. Children can climb into the truck, push the buttons, and put on the fire-fighters' hats.

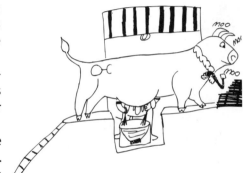

243

Playgroup Plus

Is your playgroup getting boring? Here are a few ways to spice it up:

- Turn your weekly playgroup into a potluck once a month. Have each parent bring a plate of food. Sit down and enjoy each other over a meal. Hey, it's not a restaurant, but at least the kids can play with each other while you enjoy a meal with adult company. Hire a baby-sitter!

- Incorporate a theme like bubbles, cars, colors, or animals. Have everyone bring something to do with the theme (a container of bubbles, favorite trucks/cars, or ride-on vehicles), and watch as the kids get excited about the new activities.

- Have each child bring one toy for sharing each week. Sit in a circle with children holding their own toys. Turn on music and let everyone play with his or her toy for three to five minutes. When the music stops, have them swap by passing the toys around the circle.

- Change the scenery. You can move beyond local parks and private homes. Try a gym, YMCA, or amusement park.

244

The Parent Squad

There is much to be done in a parent's day. Be creative and extend your playgroup concept to include cleaning, cooking, or other household projects. Each week choose a different house to "work on." The parent at that house gets to watch or play with all the kids while the other parents work on a project the host parent chooses. The group could clean the house, cook a meal, assemble a piece of furniture, straighten cabinets, or whatever project the parent would really like help finishing. It's funny how working in someone else's home is much more fun than working in your own.

245

Toddler Friendships

Young children will learn sharing, compassion, negotiation, and compromise from one another. Toddler friendships build self-esteem and boost creativity—and they're fun! You can encourage friendship-forming play through make-believe games that encourage role-playing or other games that require children to interact in positive ways.

* Help your little friends bond with a theme—a color they wear at the same time, special macaroni necklaces they share, or a dance they learn together.
* Put on a puppet show where each child has a part and is valued for participating.
* Play store, firehouse, house, or other group games which allow each child to attend to his own interests while participating in the group play.
* Make sure to model play time manners and sit close by to monitor interactions until the friendship is established.

246

Co-op Baby-sitting

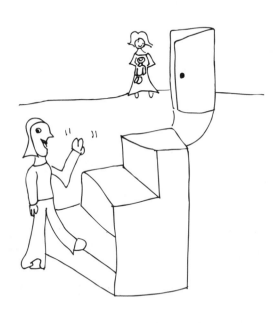

Co-op baby-sitting is different from a playgroup. A co-op is arranged as a baby-sitting option. It takes some organization, but can be very effective and successful. Here's how it works: there is a list of people who belong to the co-op. When you need a baby-sitter, you can call the co-op list of names until you find someone who is available. There is a person who keeps track of everyone's hours. If you baby-sit three hours, then the co-op owes you three hours, so you don't exactly pay the person back who baby-sat for you. Co-op baby-sitting is generally done in the home of the person doing the baby-sitting, since most people involved also have children. The co-op can be as big or small as you like. It's a good opportunity to meet other parents and save money on baby-sitting at the same time. Take some time to brainstorm ways you can organize a co-op so you can have a little time to yourself.

247

Outdoor Play: Parks and Recreation

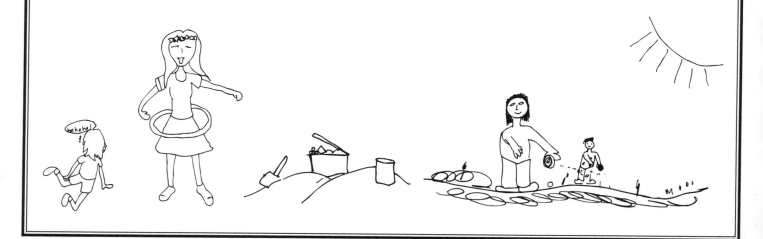

Mud Play

Age Range: 15 months and up

Materials
Dirt and water=mud
Outdoor work area
Bucket of water or hose
Small shovel or spoon
Cookie sheet

Find a place in the yard or playground where there is "clean" dirt. Cleared garden areas are ideal. Loosen a two- to three-foot area with the shovel. Add water from a hose or bucket, and mix it all up with your hands, spade, shovel, spoon, stick, or other tools.

* Make some smooshy, squishy mush. If you're brave, roll around in it, rub it on your skin, see how it feels squishing between your toes or fingers. Then hose each other off.
* Smack, stir, and push the mud around as you make figures or shapes out of the mud. Place your creations on cookie sheets, plastic lids, or a piece of wood. Decorate with sand, grass, pebbles, flower petals, and twigs. This can also be done inside if you have a large tub and don't mind cleaning up.

248

Pavement Painting

Age Range: 15 months and up

On a dry, warm day, give your child a bucket of water, one or two paint brushes, and an old sponge. Find a safe driveway, wooden deck, or piece of pavement, and let her paint large pictures or patterns with the water on the cement or wood. Pictures will dry and disappear, so there will always be more room to paint. Just refill the bucket and begin a new masterpiece as you paint away the day.

249

Sand Play

Age Range: 18 months and up

Sand picture: Fill spray bottles with water and food coloring to make the colors red, blue, green, and yellow. Flatten out the sand on the top of the sandbox by running a piece of wood or a flat stick over the top. Use the colored water spray to paint a picture in the sand. Turn the sand over and start again.

Dig for treasure: Hide objects in the sand and have your child dig for the lost treasure. Use gold spray paint to make gold nuggets out of rocks. Bury them in the sand and have your toddler go digging for gold!

Sand sculpture: Wet a pile of sand so it looks like a small hill. Make sure it is wet all the way through. Find nature objects like sticks, rocks, and feathers to stick into the sand to make a sculpture.

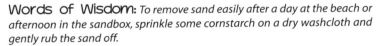

Words of Wisdom: *To remove sand easily after a day at the beach or afternoon in the sandbox, sprinkle some cornstarch on a dry washcloth and gently rub the sand off.*

—Phillip, Harrisburg, Pennsylvania

250

Water-Balloon Games

Age Range: 18 months and up

Hot potato: On a summer day when you don't mind getting wet, fill a balloon with water and poke small holes in it with a safety pin. Have your child sit across from you as you pass the balloon back and forth. You'll have lots of laughs and squeals as the water randomly squirts each player.

Water-balloon toss: Fill a few balloons with water. Hold one end of a towel as your child holds the other. The adult kneels on the grass as the child stands. Move the balloon around the towel without letting it drop to the ground. Try tossing it in the air and catching it in the towel.

Balloon crash: Fill many small water balloons with water and let your child throw them onto the pavement, against a wall, or into the air. Watch them pop when they hit the hard surface.

H$_2$O Hoops: Make a hoop with your arms and let your child try to drop or toss the balloon into the hoop.

As with all balloon activities, make sure all pieces are picked up and thrown away. Balloons are a choking hazard.

251

Sheet Design

Age Range: 21 months and up

Materials
Spray bottles
Poster or fabric paint
Old sheet
Clothesline
Clothespins

Hang the sheet on the clothesline using the clothespins. Put a rock on each corner of the sheet where it hits the ground to keep it from flapping in the wind. Fill each spray bottle half full with poster paint. Fill the rest of the bottle with water. Begin to spray the sheet with the colored paint. Use a variety of colors. Make whatever design you wish. Poster paint washes out of clothes, but fabric paint is permanent, so make sure your child is dressed accordingly. If you use fabric paint, these sheets can be used as bed decoration.

252

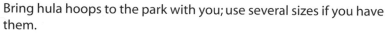

Do the Hula

Age Range: 21 months and up

Bring hula hoops to the park with you; use several sizes if you have them.

- ⚘ Use them as targets for ring, rock, or beanbag tossing.
- ⚘ Lay them out as stepping or hopping "stones" for a game of toddler hopscotch.
- ⚘ Hold them up and let your child crawl through them.
- ⚘ Use a large one for a game of horse. Stand inside the hoop with your child directly in front of you. You will hold the hula hoop up as she holds the front. Say "giddyap" as you gallop along together and "whoa" if you go too fast; take turns being horse and rider.
- ⚘ If you remember how to actually use a hula hoop, your child will be very impressed to watch it spin 'round and 'round your waist!

253

Hill Games

Age Range: 24 months and up

Hills are great fun for toddlers. Watching Mom or Dad roll down, chasing a ball to the bottom, or climbing up to begin again will be the highlight of your toddler's day. Make sure before you begin your hill play that there are no major holes on the hill, no large rocks, and no patches of poisonous or prickly plants. A grass hill is the best. Sand dunes also work, but sand can get into the mouth and eyes. Start with a ball and watch it roll down the hill, using new words and encouraging your child to repeat them. Bring many balls so you can watch them roll down all at once or one at a time. Sit at the bottom of the hill and let your child throw the balls up the hill and watch as the balls roll back down. Then show your child how to tuck his arms to his chest in preparation for rolling sideways down the hill. Walk behind your child, helping straighten him out and pushing when he stops rolling.

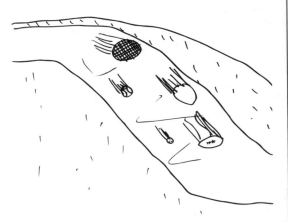

254

Shadow Fun

Age Range: 24 months and up

Shadow dancing: This is fun to do with two or more people. Have each person begin dancing as she watches her own shadow move. Then try to get your shadows to dance with each other.

Shadow tag: Instead of tagging the person, who then becomes it, you tag the shadow of the person.

Drawing shadows: Have kids make funny poses as you trace their shadows with fabric paint or markers on a sheet masking-taped to the ground. Once the outline is drawn, let the kids paint a design. Use the sheet as funky, colorful bedding afterward! This can also be done on butcher paper.

255

Sprinkler and Hose Games

Age Range: 24 months and up

Sprinkler dance: Turn the sprinkler on and encourage all the kids to dance under it. When the water is turned off, everyone stops moving. Whoever keeps moving sits down on the grass. Whoever is turning the water on and off decides who gets to sit down. The winner is the last child left standing.

Hide-and-seek tag: This is a game of tag where the sprinkler is home. Have all the kids run away from the sprinkler as the person who is "it" tries to catch them. The goal is to get back under the sprinkler before getting tagged.

Limbo: Use the hose stream as a limbo bar and encourage the kids to go under it. They can crawl, duck, or roll to get under the water. Keep lowering the stream of water, making it difficult for the kids to get under it without getting wet.

256

High Kites

Age Range: 30 months and up

Materials
Markers
Crepe paper streamers
Plastic grocery bag

Paper plates
Tape, string, twine, or yarn

Long before your child is able to fly a kite on his own, he will be fascinated with kites when he sees them flying in the sky. Parks with large, open, grassy areas tend to attract kite-fliers. Help your child make a kite to hold and run with.

Paper-plate kite: Attach a string to the back of a paper plate with tape, or poke two holes near the center and run the string through and knot it. Tape on colorful streamers for the kite's tail. Then hold the string and run with it. This kind of kite doesn't fly high in the sky; it simply blows in the wind behind your toddler. Draw designs or a face on the plate to decorate. Plain crepe paper cut into streamers is fun to wave in the wind all by itself.

Grocery-bag kite: Tie the handles of a plastic shopping bag together with the end of a ball of string (or a roll of kite string). Staple or tape a few two-foot lengths of ribbon to the bottom of the bag for kite tails. Run around the park in the wind. As the bag fills with air, it will start to fly, and you can let out string as it dives and soars.

257

Flowering Names

Age Range: 30 to 36 months

Materials
Wildflower seeds
Stick
Garden plot or window box filled with dirt

Prepare the soil of a section of the garden at least four by three feet by removing stones, weeds, and other debris. Use the stick to write your child's name in the soil, making the grooves one inch deep. You can also draw a simple design or shape. Evenly sprinkle the wildflower seeds into the lines. Instead of covering the seeds with soil, simply press them into the grooves with your hands. Water lightly every other day. Your child will be able to see his name or design growing as the seedlings appear and then grow into flowers.

258

Outdoor Obstacle Course

Age Range: 30 to 36 months

Materials

Old tires or hula hoops
Laundry baskets

Jump rope
Cardboard boxes or cartons

Set up an obstacle course for your child using equipment from the house and yard. Your child should have obstacles to go under, over, through, around, inside, and outside. Colored yarn or chalk can be used as a path for him to follow. In the beginning, have him simply walk through the course, following the yarn through each section. Once your child knows the way and what to do at each obstacle, you might time him or clap your hands and count how long it takes for him to get to the end. Make sure Mom or Dad tries it, too!

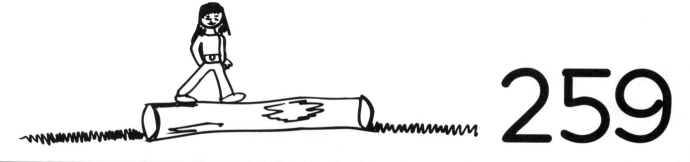

259

Pipe Forts

Age Range: 36 months and up

Materials
White PVC pipe (found at building supply stores and usually used for irrigation systems)
Various joints for the pipe

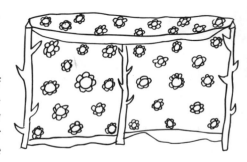

You will want to buy at least one hundred feet of pipe and a variety of joints so you can put the fort together at various angles. If you have a particular design in mind, such as a teepee or house, you may want to draw up a plan before cutting the pipe. Use a hacksaw to cut pieces of four- or five-foot lengths, or whatever length your design requires. Push the pieces of pipe into the joints according to whatever shape you wish to create. Once the structure is standing, use old sheets, blankets, or fabric scraps to create outer walls. The pieces of pipe can be taken apart and used over and over.

260

Backyard Beasts

Protect your child from the sun and bug bites with these tips.

To avoid bug bites:

❈ Dress your child appropriately: wear light-colored clothing (bright colors attract bugs); if walking in brush, wear long pants, long-sleeved shirts, socks, and shoes. Make sure your child does not wash with scented soaps or use scented lotions, which also attract bugs.

❈ Be wary of sunscreen–insect repellent combinations. These are fine for one application, but re-applying, which you may need to do for the sunscreen, may cause overexposure to DEET (an ingredient in most bug repellents).

❈ Treat minor bug bites promptly by applying an ice cube to reduce the swelling and minimize itching. Hydrocortisone cream can also be used.

❈ Extreme swelling, trouble breathing, hives, swollen tongue, headache, or nausea may indicate a life-threatening allergic reaction to bug bites—in these cases, seek immediate medical attention.

To protect kids from the sun:

❈ Use a total protection approach, which includes using a broad-spectrum waterproof sunscreen of SPF 15 or higher and wearing protective clothing like hats, sunglasses, and other clothing designed to screen out the sun. Also avoid direct sunlight whenever possible between 10 A.M. and 4 P.M.

❈ Put sunscreen on your child before he goes outside—most sunscreens take fifteen minutes before they begin to work.

❈ Even if your sunscreen claims to last all day and is waterproof, re-apply it at least once during the day.

261

Parties and Celebrations

Party Tips

1. Schedule the party for no more than ninety minutes in length.
2. Invite one parent to stay with each child.
3. Have an activity set up and ready to go so kids have something to do while they wait for the others to arrive. Play dough, pipe-cleaner sculptures, balls, bubbles, and sidewalk chalk are good entertainers.
4. Hold the party outdoors if possible.
5. Invite as many guests as the child is years old.
6. Give prizes or favors to the kids while the birthday person is opening his presents. Stickers, coloring books, beanbags, squeeze toys, toy cars, ice-cream–cone certificates, and glow sticks are all good choices.
7. If planning on having a piñata, look for the kind that has a ribbon to pull that lets the candy fall out. (Toddlers may have a hard time hitting it hard enough to break it open.)
8. Plan some group physical activities, even if it is simply running around, jumping, or dancing.

262

Party Fare

Age Range: 15 months and up

Determining what foods to serve at toddler parties can be difficult. Here are some ideas and tips:

* Make a pizza. Ask your pizza parlor to make up the pizzas with dough and sauce, leaving any extra ingredients on the side. Have the children add the cheese and other toppings themselves. They'll eat a far better variety when they're the ones putting the toppings on! You can also buy the pizza base at the grocery store.
* Serve food that children can pick up with their hands, like chicken tenders, tater tots, pizza snacks, and small burritos.
* Skewered anything is fun—fruit, vegetables, cheese, sandwich meats, or grilled chicken. Make sure to buy dull skewers or use straws.
* Prepare individual boxed or bagged lunches in advance—sandwiches shaped with cookie cutters, Jell-O, yogurt, applesauce, fruit cups, string cheese, raisins, trail mix, pretzels, juice boxes, etc. Don't forget napkins. There's no work required but handing them out!
* Prepare a build-your-own-cupcake bar—set out unfrosted cupcakes along with several kinds of frosting, or you can add food coloring to vanilla frosting to make several colors. Use Popsicle sticks to spread the icing. Include all sorts of toppings like sprinkles, gummy bears, and M&Ms. You can do the same with ice-cream sundaes.
* If you are having cake and ice cream, scoop ice cream into paper cupcake liners and freeze before the party to make serving easier.
* Be sensitive to possible food allergies—consider asking parents when they RSVP if there are any dietary restrictions.

263

Decorative Ice Bucket

Materials
Empty cardboard milk carton
Bottle of vodka (to use as a mold since vodka doesn't freeze)
Decorations

Open the top of the empty milk carton. Put the bottle of Vodka into the milk carton and fill the carton halfway with water. Have your child add little toys, fresh flowers, marbles or whatever decoration fits the theme of your party. Freeze. Then fill the carton to the top with water and add more decorations. Freeze again. When solid and ready to use, pull the vodka bottle out. It may take a few minutes to loosen the bottle and peel the cardboard carton off the outside of the mold. You now have a decorative ice bucket. Place in a bowl or on a tray to catch the drips.

Words of Wisdom: *We've started making our own wrapping paper by writing the recipient's name many times and in many fonts on our computer and then printing each name out on large address labels. We wrap the presents in white butcher paper and then use the name stickers to decorate.*

—Rhonda, Chandler, Arizona

264

Thank-You Notes

Age Range: 15 months and up

Teaching good manners is part of a parent's job. Whenever your child receives a present of any kind, get in the habit of sending thank-you notes.

* Take a picture of your child with the gift and make a thank-you card out of the picture by gluing it to a plain piece of construction paper folded in half.
* Make personal handprint stationery. Have your child dip his hand in paint and stamp it onto a blank sheet of paper. Once the paint has dried, you can write the thank you over the top or all around the outside of the hand.
* For relatives who live far away and send a gift, consider making a cassette tape giving a description of the birthday party—the people who attended, the games played, and funny things your child did. Finish the tape by thanking them for the present. Make duplicates.

••

Words of Wisdom: *If we are ordering pizza for a party, I ask the restaurant to arrange some of the toppings into the shape of the child's age.*
—Jeff, Brigham City, Utah

265

Group Games

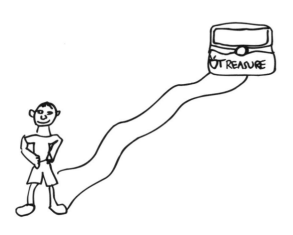

Treasure hunt: Hide a treasure, which is a box filled with candy, plastic jewelry, or other party favors. Draw out pictures to show the child where she should go to find the next clue (also a picture). Give each child the first clue at the same time.

Group draw: Tape a long piece of butcher paper to the floor and let all the kids draw or finger-paint on it.

Spaghetti wiggle: Cook three packages of spaghetti. Mix spaghetti, ½ cup vegetable oil, and food coloring of your choice and put it into a child's wading pool. Let the children play in it.

Parachute: Use a big sheet or store-bought parachute to play all sorts of circle games. Raise the parachute in the air and have kids hide under it, roll a ball around on the top, make waves, or hold onto the edges and march around in a circle.

266

Sibling Party

Age Range: 15 months and up

This is a special party planned for the older sibling of the toddler. Toddlers tend to take much of Mom or Dad's energy, so this is a special party planned with the intent to make the older sibling king or queen of the moment. Hire a baby-sitter to watch your toddler. Invite a bunch of your older child's friends over for this party, which has no purpose but to focus on your older child. Make his favorite snacks, go someplace fun, or pick a favorite theme—whatever will make your older child feel special. You may also want to plan this party as a surprise. If you have many friends who have toddlers as well as older children, make this a group event where all the older children are invited while the toddlers are either left at home or watched at the party house by a hired baby-sitter.

267

Car and Truck Party

Age Range: 15 months and up

Things that roll delight most toddlers. Make invitations out of construction paper in the shape of cars or trucks. Take a photo of your child in the front seat of your car pretending to drive. Copy this photo onto paper. Glue this picture of your child in the window of the car or truck on the invitation. Ask each child to bring a favorite large riding car, a truck, or any toy that rolls.

* Set up a vehicle obstacle course specially designed for push cars or trucks. One of the parents can lead the way through the course in follow-the-leader style with each child following behind, directing his own truck or car.
* Create a city by taping a long piece of butcher paper to the floor and drawing roads, railroad tracks, and city locations. Let the kids drive their small cars through the city. Make sure to have a supply of small matchbox-sized cars to drive around the city.
* If you know people who own vintage cars, ask them to come by and give the kids a ride around the block.

268

Tea Party

Age Range: 18 months and up

Little girls love tea parties. Use a child-sized table, set with all the necessary items: flowers, cookies, sugar cubes, teacups, and plates. Invite guests to bring their favorite teddy bears or dolls to accompany them as guests. Make small tea sandwiches, tiny cookies, or finger food. Serve raspberry tea. Mothers can serve the girls as if they were in a fancy restaurant, using a real menu. Before the girls begin enjoying the tea, you might want to decorate hats to wear to the fancy event. Buy a straw hat for each girl at a craft store. Use feathers, silk flowers, ribbons, and bows to decorate the hats. Items will need to be glued on with a hot glue gun, so mothers will have to help by gluing items where children place them.

....

Words of Wisdom: *Put the party favors and candy gifts in a basket. Attach helium balloons. As the children remove the favors, the basket rises like a hot air balloon.*

—Patty, York, Nebraska

269

Bubble Party

Age Range: 24 months and up

Everything about this party is going to be bubble fun from the invitations to the last good-bye!

- Print or write out invitations and then have your child blow bubbles onto it—as they hit and pop, you create bubble art!
- Make up a bubbly punch by adding sherbet to clear soda.
- Make up your own bubble solution (one cup water, two tablespoons light Karo syrup or Glycerin, four tablespoons dishwashing liquid and food coloring) to use in bubble games.
- Let the kids blow bubbles, catch the bubbles blown by others, make their own big bubbles, see who can pop the most bubbles, etc.
- Turn on music and tell them to act like bubbles floating up and down, popping on the ground.
- Fill plastic tubs with water and dishwashing soap to create a pile of bubbles to use in making bubble sculptures.

270

Fishy Party

Age Range: 24 months and up

- Cut out invitations in the shape of fish.
- Use fish bowls as serving bowls. Prepare several boxes of blue Jell-O as directed, except use a fish bowl. Cool in refrigerator for about an hour, until partially set. Add gummy fish all around, pushing some into the Jell-O. Return to fridge to fully set.
- Make fish-shaped sandwiches or pizza by cutting dough or bread in the shape of fish before covering with cheese or sauce.
- Go fishing. Attach a string to a wooden dowel. Tie a magnet to the end of the string. Put prizes into a baby pool or tub behind a curtain or cardboard wall of some kind so the kids can't see what kind of prize they might get. Attach paper clips to the prizes so the magnet can hold the prize on the end of the line. A parent will need to sit behind the cardboard to stick a prize to each magnet.
- Use a blue fabric sheet to create a river and encourage kids to wiggle in the river, pretending to be fish. Some of the kids can pretend to be in a boat floating on top of the river, catching the fish!

271

Spring Is Here

Age Range: 24 months and up

Prepare box breakfasts on a Friday or Saturday night. They might include small cartons of milk or juice, muffins, hard-boiled eggs, or yogurt. Include a special note to each person. Before everyone gets up, hide the breakfasts outside in the garden. Leave a note on the kitchen table letting everyone know they must search for their breakfasts. If children cannot read, wait for them to walk into the kitchen, then tell everyone at the same time to begin the search. Also hide packets of flower and vegetable seeds or bulbs to be found and planted. Set up an outdoor table and eat breakfast together. After breakfast, plant the seeds and bulbs in the garden.

272

Garden Party

Age Range: 24 months and up

Send seed packets as invitations. Cut out a piece of construction paper to write the party information and glue it to the flower packet.

Flower favors: Take a round-ball lollipop and wrap a piece of yellow tissue paper over it to form the center of the flower. Cut a bunch of big teardrop-shaped petals out of colored tissue paper. Secure the petals together, fanned all around the lollipop stick, with floral tape. These can also be used as party centerpieces sticking in a flowerpot filled with foam.

Serve fruit bouquets: Stick fruit onto straws or dull skewers—cut in balls or use canapé cutters—and place them in a terra-cotta pot filled with foam.

Flower cake: Make a regular nine-by-thirteen–inch cake, leaving enough batter to make six cupcakes as well. Bake both the cake and pan of six cupcakes. Frost the cake with white frosting. Attach the cupcakes to the upper two-thirds of the cake by putting icing on the bottom and sticking them to the cake. Ice the cupcakes with white icing and decorate with lifesaver Gummies, sprinkles, M&M Minis, and Jujyfruits. Use green gel icing to make flower stems, grass, and leaves.

Flower masks: Use a two-by-twenty-four–inch strip of construction paper. Hold the strip up to the outside of each child's face. Tape or staple the ends together to fit snuggly in the shape of an oval when slipped onto your child's face. Cut petals out of colored construction paper. Tape the petals to the strip and then bend them so they stick directly out from the face.

273

Moving Party

Age Range: 30 months and up

Sometimes a family has to move out of an area. Help your child say good-bye to friends.

- Use your moving announcement as an invitation.
- Put the moving boxes together in advance. Set out trays of paint and let the kids paint the outside of the boxes.
- Tape a large piece of butcher paper to the floor with a drawing of where your new home will be located in relation to your present location. Let the kids use small cars or planes to trace the road or air route to your new house.
- Make sure to take lots of pictures and get duplicates so you can send copies to your child's friends.
- Give each child a good-bye letter, a few self-addressed envelopes with stamps on them for your new house location, and crayons for writing. Hopefully your child will receive many letters within weeks of your move.

274

Father's Day Fashion Show

Age Range: 30 months and up

Invite all the dads to attend this party. Have the dads and kids dress up in fun, gaudy costumes or outfits the moms bring or put together in advance. Make a construction-paper crown for Dad to wear while modeling his fashions. Encourage Dad to work with his child to create some sort of routine or dance they do together while out on the makeshift runway. Serve hotdogs, chips, dip, and soda. Make sure to videotape the fashion show.

Words of Wisdom: *I've started making a cupcake with a single candle for each young birthday party guest along with the birthday cake. That way, when it's time to blow out the candles, they can all get in on the action without overwhelming or disappointing the birthday boy or girl—and it makes for great photos, too!*

—Amelia, Crofton, Maryland

275

Section Four:
Family Time

Family Fun

New Traditions

A tradition is simply a customary way of doing something that is handed down through family or community. Traditions don't have to be old; they can be started today in your family. Take some time to think about traditions that were in your family of origin. Make a list of traditions you would like to pass down, and think about new possibilities. Here are a few ideas:

Special outings: Take your daughter to tea at a fancy restaurant every year—maybe on or around her birthday or Mother's Day; or take your son to a baseball game or for a ride on a train.

Sharing time after dinner: Make the time after dinner a sharing time by inviting family members to talk about their days, or in the case of children, show what they've made.

Family field trips: Kids look forward to unusual adventures that stray from the schedule they follow on most days. There are many family-friendly locations in most communities—the zoo, the park (which might have live music), children's museums, or art galleries. Make a tradition of going somewhere special one Saturday a month.

276

Memory Lane

Set aside some time to share memories together as a family. Watch home videos or look through picture albums. Let your children tell you what they remember; afterward the adults can fill in forgotten details. Moments we set aside to share common experiences strengthen bonds and create a sense of security for everyone.

....

Words of Wisdom: *Name and date baby pictures. Believe it or not, memories do fade, and when there is more than one child, sometimes confusion arises.*

—Sandy, Galesburg, Illinois

277

Play Hooky

Every once in a while it rejuvenates the soul to play hooky. Call in sick to work or forget the housework and take the day off to do something fun. When everyone else is working or at school, places that are usually packed are relatively empty. Invite grandparents to join in the fun.

··

Words of Wisdom: *I remember one morning my mother came into my room before school and asked me if I would like to go skiing with her instead of going to school. I felt so lucky, like it was my birthday or some special event. That memory stuck in my head and taught me more about life than a year of school.*

—Sheila, Portola Valley, California

278

Create Family Stationery

Use your child's drawings when designing family stationery. First take a black fine-tip marker and draw over the lines in the drawing if they were drawn in pencil or crayon. Then take the drawing to a copy store and reduce the size of the image to whatever size works for your stationery design. Cut the image out and glue it onto a blank piece of paper. Use other design elements that represent your family; perhaps the faces of family members, a drawing of your house or yard, or each person's name written around the page as a border. Once your stationery is designed, make copies on different colored paper and get ready for your first mailing.

Words of Wisdom: *One year we took an old refrigerator box, opened it up, and painted a scene on it so that each person's head could stick through one of the oval holes we cut—kind of like the ones you see at amusement parks. We used that picture for our holiday cards, and then later transferred it to the bottom of family stationery.*

—Joseph, Erie, Pennsylvania

279

Vacation Memories

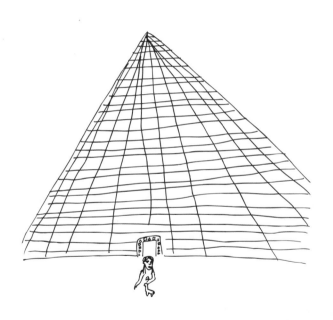

Next time you go on vacation and leave the kids at home, make sure to pack one of each of your children's favorite stuffed animals. When out exploring your vacation spot, take pictures of their stuffed animals at various locations. Mom or Dad might hold one of the animals, place it on a statue, or compose a funny scene. Surprise the kids with the pictures when you return home. Your kids will also be more interested in where you went and what you did if their favorite animals are in the pictures. Beware—your suitcase will be filled with stuffed animals from then on!

···

Words of Wisdom: *When I travel I carry some of my kids' favorite books with me, so when I call them at night from my hotel room, I can still read them a bedtime story.*

—Mike, Portage, Indiana

280

Play Silly Games

Silly games that allow everyone to participate build family unity. Here are a few favorites:

Shrinking sheet: Put a sheet on the floor or grass. Everyone in the family has to try to fit on the sheet, lying down without any body part falling over the edge. If everyone fits, then fold the sheet or blanket and try again. See how small you can make the blanket and still fit.

Wolf in the woods: Pretend the living room is a forest with one wolf and several other animals running around. One person is the wolf; everyone else pretends to be other forest animals. The other animals lie on the forest floor perfectly still with their eyes wide open (tired parents love this game!). No moving is allowed except for breathing, blinking, and eye movement. You're out of the game if the wolf catches you moving in any other way. The wolf is allowed to try to get the other animals to move any way she can without touching them: by making funny faces, making strange sounds, or telling them jokes, etc.

281

Make Mealtime Special

Age Range: 24 months and up

With a little extra effort you can make mealtime a special family memory for your child.

- Make (or buy) folded "tent" place cards. Write the names of all dinner guests (even if it's just the usual few!) and let your child embellish by gluing on colorful buttons, dried pasta, rickrack, or bows.
- Light candles for everyday meals—even during the day. Keep them out of reach, of course, but make sure to let the kids blow them out when the meal is over.
- Play background music. Classical music sets a calm mood, but it is also fun to play silly songs, jazz, or rock music.
- Turn off the TV. Eating in front of the TV isn't an event; eating like it matters and you care about being together makes every meal special. It doesn't have to be a fancy meal to feel like a family celebration.

282

Hands of Time

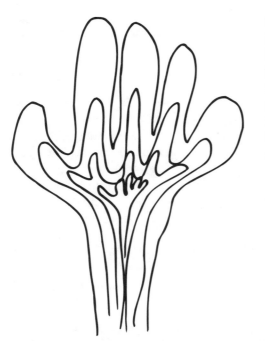

Use colored construction paper to make foot and hand cutouts. Pick one color for each member of the family. Once you've outlined each foot and hand, cut them out. Take a piece of construction paper in a color different from all the foot and hand cutouts. Glue the largest cutout to the piece of paper and work up to the smallest, which is then glued on the top. Line them up by either the palms or the heels. Put a date on the bottom and frame it. When your first child turns eighteen, do it again, making sure to use the same colors for each person that were used the first time.

••

Words of Wisdom: *I used to think my mom was really silly for saving so many things: our artwork, letters, hand prints we'd made in preschool. Now that I have my own child, I love looking at the things I did at her age.*
—Pat, Salt Lake City, Utah

283

Between Us

Develop a family signal—something you can do inconspicuously that says, "I love you" without actually saying, "I love you." Maybe it's three squeezes to the hand or a wave of a pinky finger—whatever it is, you can express your feelings with it without saying a word. This is great when children get older and less comfortable with public parental displays of affection. Once the kids understand the concept of hand signals and begin to use them, you may want to develop a few more. Here are some worth developing: please stop interrupting, we'll leave in a minute, no, you're being so kind, please help me, or stop.

284

The Family That Cooks Together

Pick a day to cook for the entire week. Many parents say that mealtime is the worst time of the day with toddlers; imagine how you'd feel if all you had to do was take a dish out of the freezer. Plus, you'll only have to clean up the kitchen once. Concentrate on making bulk meals like soup, chili, lasagna, or meatballs to freeze in batches for busier mealtimes. You may also want to prepare fresh meals for two days to leave in the refrigerator. Encourage everyone to help in a relaxed atmosphere as you work together as a team. You'll have a lot more patience to let your toddler "help" than you might on a busy, hungry weeknight.

285

Backyard Camping

Toddlers love to camp. They like the whole idea of setting up a tent, slumbering in sleeping bags, and cooking dinner over a campfire. The backyard is just as exciting as any campground and much more convenient.

- Pitch a tent and lay out the sleeping bags. Serve hot dogs, beans, and s'mores.
- Listen for all the night sounds you normally don't hear while in the house.
- Make owl masks out of paper plates with feathers and yarn. Pretend to be night owls while you sing campfire songs and read stories.
- Attach bells to the zipper of your tent exit so your kids can't escape unnoticed. A bell on the child isn't a bad idea, either!
- Bring a flashlight for each child. They love to shine them in the tent after dark. Play light tag on the ceiling or check outside when you hear animal sounds.
- Don't forget the glow sticks so the kids can glow in the dark, or citronella candles so they don't get eaten alive by mosquitoes.
- Keep an ongoing camping journal that everyone contributes to. Store it with your camping equipment.

286

Topsy Turvy

Spice up your days by mixing them up!

* Eat dessert first one night (just don't expect them to eat a healthy dinner afterward!).
* Have breakfast for dinner and dinner for breakfast.
* Walk, take a bus, or, better yet, take a cab instead of driving to the store.
* Make an unbirthday cake and wear party hats when you blow out the candles together.
* Say "goodnight" when you wake up, and read a goodnight story before you get out of bed in the morning.
* Read a storybook backwards, or read it forwards but change the ending or have the child make up the ending!

287

Game Night

Dedicate a certain night a week to games. In the beginning, you may just be coloring or putting puzzles together, but in no time you'll be playing board games and card games and putting together model airplanes. Game night will become a tradition, teaching your kids the joy of spending quality, entertaining time with one another.

Words of Wisdom: *We pretend the electricity is out one night each week. There's no TV and no stereo to distract us. We light candles (out of reach), tell stories, play games, and sing songs—it is the best night of the week.*
—Mindy, Peachtree City, Georgia

288

Here, Fido

Materials
1 1/2 cups whole-wheat flour
1/2 cup wheat germ
1 tablespoon dark brown sugar
1/4 cup raisins (optional)
1 1/4 cups smooth peanut butter
3/4 cup milk

Make homemade dog biscuits for the family's favorite canine companion. Preheat oven to 375°F (190ºC). Line cookie sheets with parchment. Combine flour, wheat germ, sugar, and raisins. With electric mixer, beat peanut butter and milk together until blended. With the mixer on low speed, gradually add the flour mixture and beat until just combined. Turn the dough out onto a lightly floured board and knead lightly. Roll out about 1/3-inch thick. Cut into shapes. Transfer to cookie sheets. Bake for ten to twelve minutes or until slightly browned. Let the biscuits cool on the sheets. Store well-wrapped at room temperature for two to three days or refrigerate or freeze. Makes about three dozen three-inch dog bones.

289

Concrete Stepping Stone

Materials

A two-inch–high mold: plastic planter saucer from the garden shop, stepping stone mold from a craft store, old cake pan, etc.

Stepping stone concrete (available at craft stores)

Embellishments: seashells, marbles, glass beads and gems, mosaic tiles, buttons, small toys, or mementos

Popsicle sticks for writing

Patio/outdoor paint

Old screen cut one inch smaller than the shape of your stone

Set your mold on the work surface and prepare the concrete mix according to directions. The consistency should be like soft cookie dough—scoopable but not pourable. Scoop it into the mold, filling it halfway. Smooth it down and lay your screening material over it. Continue filling the goop to the top. Gently tap the outside of the mold to remove air bubbles and even out the concrete, and then don't move it again! Let it set for thirty to sixty minutes. Then start decorating. You may want to begin with a foot or hand print. If you make a mistake, you can always smooth it over using a Popsicle stick or spoon and begin again. When finished, let it sit for three days undisturbed. Once dry, pop it out of the mold. You can also paint it with outdoor patio paint and then seal it with an acrylic sealer. Let sit another week before placing outside or walking on the stone.

290

Sibling Games

Tips to Facilitate Sibling Play

Whether your toddler is the younger sibling or by now the older one, there are ways to develop a strong friendship between them.

Don't compare them: Praise each child for what you love about her, for her own accomplishments, making sure each child knows she is valued for herself and not because she does something better or worse than a sibling.

Create a team spirit: Get your kids doing things together, even if it is a simple task like picking up the trash in the car. If they are working well together, throw in a reward they didn't expect like making cookies or going to the park.

Teach empathy: When one of your children has been hurt, model the behavior you want the other child to learn. Walk over together, pat the hurt child on the back, let your toddler help you clean and bandage the wound or get a glass of water or an ice pack. Point out how much you appreciate the child's caring behavior.

Let them teach each other: The child who is teaching gains self-esteem from being needed, and the one learning gets to see that his sibling cares enough to help him.

291

Family Puppets

Give your older child a disposable camera. He is the head photographer while the younger child is the assistant (who also gets to take pictures). Ask them to take pictures of all family members. Once the pictures are developed, cover them with contact paper, cut them out, and glue them to Popsicle sticks. Let the older sibling help your toddler to recognize family names as they play together with the puppets.

Words of Wisdom: *When my daughter was born, I gave my son a disposable camera to take photos at the hospital. He did an amazing job of capturing everything and everyone. They're real treasures in our scrapbook, and he felt very important being the dedicated cameraman!*

—Pete, Sykesville, Maryland

292

Ready, Set, Go

Toddlers love to jump off of things. Show your older child how to hold his sister's hands while she jumps off a box or step. Say, "Ready, set, go" and then jump. Toddlers like to anticipate when they are supposed to do something, so the ready, set, go chant can also be used while doing other things like hopping, sitting down, jumping up, or any other movement the older sibling wants to make up.

Words of Wisdom: *I have my two-year-old daughter draw special pictures to hang over the new baby's crib, and then I make sure she sees how much her little brother admires them. I use plastic sheet protectors so she can create new masterpieces whenever she likes.*

—Alexa, Bedford, Massachusetts

293

Peekaboo Faces

Cut peek holes for your toddler's eyes on one side of a shoebox. Cut a rectangular window on the opposite side. Have your toddler hold up the box and look through the peek holes while his sibling makes a face. The rectangular window will frame his sibling's face and make it look like a picture. Try a game where every time you clap, the sibling changes facial expression or body shape. The faster you clap, the funnier it looks through the peek holes. Switch places.

294

Food Projects

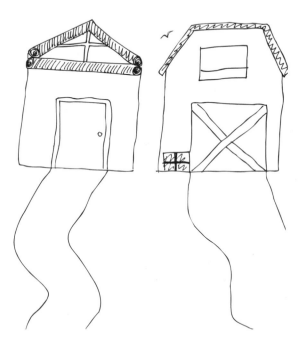

Painted cookies: Colored egg yolk makes a glossy edible paint on the top of plain sugar cookies. Use one egg yolk mixed with one teaspoon of water and a few drops of food coloring. Paint the sugar cookies before baking, then bake as usual.

Pretzel forts: You will need a small, clean box the size of a milk carton, thick stick pretzels, and peanut butter. Spread a moderate amount of peanut butter onto the sides of the box. Design the walls and roof using the pretzels. Bite them down to size for exact patterning.

Jell-O faces: Fill small individual glass bowls with instant pudding or Jell-O. Let kids make faces on the pudding or Jell-O with string licorice or gummy worms for hair, raisins, M&Ms, or gummy candy for mouths.

Group Outings

Train or bus ride: Kids of all ages are excited to experiment with all modes of transportation. There is so much to see, hear, and learn—from getting tickets, to watching fellow passengers—there is never a dull moment.

Pet store: Kids can spend hours in a pet store watching the fish, lizards, rats, hamsters, birds, cats, and other pets. Let the older sibling tell the younger one what she knows about the creatures they see. When your toddler asks questions, ask the big sister if she knows the answer.

Construction site: After watching workers and their machines, your kids can come home and play in the sand with their own dump trucks, shovels, and cranes.

296

Camping In

Let your kids plan a sleepover in one another's bedroom or in the family room. Bring sleeping bags and maybe even a small tent if there's room. Make popcorn. Sit in a circle and tell stories before bed, or ask the kids to put on a puppet or dance show together. And don't forget the all-important flashlights!

....

Words of Wisdom: *I've created one specific job that each sibling is responsible for that's related to helping another sibling (tying shoes, reading a story, helping Mom and Dad with the baby's bath, etc.). It promotes cooperation and kindness—and it helps us!*

—Allen, Center Point, Iowa

297

Preparing for a New Baby

* When mommy's tummy starts to obviously show, let your toddler feel the baby moving and kicking, but don't force him to be interested.
* Have him help you decorate the nursery.
* Talk about what will happen when you actually have the baby and how it will be for him. "Grandma will take you to preschool and then bring you to the hospital, etc".
* Help him select a present for the baby when she comes, and be sure to tuck one away for him!
* Bring him to the hospital as soon after the birth as possible and let him meet the new baby and pass out favors to visitors.
* Let him be the dedicated new-baby gift opener.
* Involve him whenever possible (if he's interested—don't push it) in newborn care (baths, diaper changes, stroller-pushing). Buy him a baby of his own so he can do exactly what you are doing with his own baby.
* Be sure to devote some big-boy time for just you and him.

298

Random Kindness

Keep a random kindness jar for each child. Have each child decorate her jar with stickers, paint, markers, and glitter. Any time you catch the kids in a random act of kindness, reward them with a decorative sticker. Write what they did on a construction paper heart and put it into the jar. At the end of the day or week at a special time, read the kind acts each child offered. You'll love seeing your kids become conscious of their actions towards one another.

299

Sibling Theme Days

Brothers and sisters become friends and learn to enjoy each other when they share fun experiences.

Backward day: Wear clothes backwards, eat meals backwards, do what you do at night in the morning, have a backwards walking race, etc.

Color day: Everyone wears clothes the designated color. Food, drink, and bath water all match that day's color. Food coloring can transform foods like scrambled eggs, milk, mashed potatoes, and pasta.

Wild hair day: This is the day where the curlers, hairspray, hair gel, and wacky barrettes come out. Ask your older child to help make your toddler's hair wacky. Parents can participate in this event; just don't plan to leave the house!

Pajama day: Everyone wears pajamas all day.

Sing please day: Every question or request has to be sung.

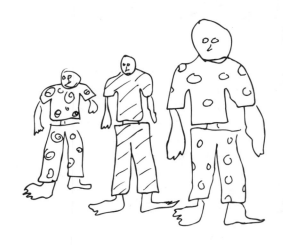

300

Potpourri Shapes

Materials
Large heart- or other-shaped cookie cutter
Wax paper
Large bowl
Colorful potpourri (small pieces like lavender work best)
White school glue
Twine, string, or ribbon

Drizzle the glue into the potpourri, mixing until the potpourri is well coated and the mixture is about the consistency of Rice Krispy Treats. Set the cookie cutter on top of the wax paper and fill it halfway with the potpourri mixture. Fold the twine into a loop and lay the two ends of the loop on top of the mixture, making sure to leave the loop end sticking out. Continue filling the cookie cutter with potpourri mixture. Pack the mixture tightly before slowly lifting off the cookie cutter. Let dry fully. Wash the bowl and cookie cutter immediately with warm, soapy water.

301

Bag Skits

Materials
Large paper bags
Various household items for props

This is a fun group activity for siblings. Ask someone who is not playing to put eight to ten props into the large paper bag—things like a dustpan, underwear, wig, rag, toy, or anything else you can find. Once the bag is full, give it to the kids and ask them to make up a skit using all the props in the bag. The props do not have to be used according to what they are. For example, underwear can become a hat, the dust pan might be a sled, and the rag a baby. Sit and watch the silly things your kids come up with.

302

Special Parent Day

Why wait until Mother's or Father's Day to express appreciation? Once a month, help your children work together to lavish a parent with treats such as breakfast in bed, a homemade card, a clean car, or something else that parent might appreciate. Take turns being the chosen parent! Help your children to plan the day's activities with the parent in mind. This will foster cooperation and a sense of joy in giving, as well as give your children something to work on together.

303

Kitchen Table Landscape

Materials
Vegetables
Clean blue plastic place mats

Here's a sure way to get all your kids to eat their vegetables. Cut peppers, cauliflower (clouds), broccoli (trees), carrots (house), radishes, and herbs into various-sized pieces, making sure that one side is flat. Put the vegetables in the middle of the table within reach of all children. Give each child his or her own place mat. Let the older sibling show the younger how to make a design on his own place mat, helping if needed. Once the designs are complete, make sure to praise each child's effort before suggesting that the feasting begin. Bring out a variety of dips: ranch dressing or a mix of half peanut butter and half yogurt are favorites. Make sure to get a picture of both siblings with their creations.

304

Silly Manners

Teaching kids to have good manners is easy with a sense of humor. Here are a few ideas to get your children saying their pleases and thank-yous, helping and complimenting each other:

Speed please: Whenever your kids say please to you, do that task with exaggerated speed and silliness. If they forget to say please, stand in place until they remember.

Play that scene again: When your kids are mean to each other, simply say, "Take two," and then ask them to repeat what they've just done being kind or helpful to each other. The kids will get so tired of doing it over that they'll begin to think about the action before they do it.

Meditation minute: When the kids begin arguing over a toy or some other item, call for a meditation minute. Both the kids have to sit on the floor, not talk to each other, put the toy aside, and take ten audible breaths.

305

Grandparenting

Food for Thought

It's funny how parents just don't seem to feed kids things they like, but at Grandma and Grandpa's house the food is great! To enhance this experience, instead of shopping before the grandkids arrive, wait until they're with you. Plan the menu together, then go to the store and pick out a few things. Let each child pick out a box of cereal to be their own and write their name on the box with a thick marker. Even with foods you're sure they liked on the last visit, Mom might have changed the brand, or the kids may have moved on to a new favorite. So, at the very least, make sure to inquire beforehand what food to purchase. It's not fun to be stuck with a lot of food that the kids won't eat!

306

Your Pace

For some grandparents, it's the calm and lack of rushing that come with age and retirement that will attract your grandchildren to you. You will be a retreat from their otherwise hectic lives. For other grandparents, it's the cool, fast-paced, savvy lives you lead that will make you hip in the eyes of your grandkids. Be who you are—your grandkids will appreciate it. Also, take time to focus on what you have that parents don't—pets, garden, etc. If you have a special hobby—like painting, car collecting, or cooking—allow your grandchildren to share your joy. That will make time with you all the more special and memorable.

Words of Wisdom: *I used to catch a cold every time my grandkids came to visit until I showed them how to cough and sneeze into their elbows or shoulders to lessen the spread of germs by hand.*

—Nancy, Laredo, Texas

307

Establish a Play Area

If grandchildren will be spending time at your house, there are a few things you can do that will make visits more fun for everyone.

❀ Start a separate cabinet where craft supplies are stored. It should contain crayons, paper, play dough, finger paint, old boxes, wrapping paper scraps, scissors, a glue stick, old magazines, old socks, and felt.

❀ Start a dress-up box. As you do your yearly closet-cleaning, save the old jackets, dresses, high-heeled shoes, jewelry, hats, and ties. Consider cutting the dress bottoms and coat arms to a reasonable length.

❀ Try to clean an area and designate it as a play area. Even a small area will do. This way there will be no excuse for having toys all over the house! Buy a cheap wall mirror and hang it up in this area, then watch the children find a million uses for it.

❀ For inexpensive and instant room decoration the children will love, take a few photos of the kids and blow them up to poster size. Then, buy cheap plastic poster frames and hang them in the room where the children sleep.

308

Special Books

Do you remember any of the books that were read to you as a child? Do you remember the special books you read to your children? Start reading those books to your grandchildren. Tell them how you used to read them to their mom or dad. Tell them little things you remember, like how their dad loved this character or was afraid of that one, or that their mother started dressing her stuffed animals just like the heroine. You may want to record yourself reading these stories along with your grandchildren's questions and responses to the stories you tell so the tapes can be played when you are not with them!

309

Stay in Touch

Color connection: Buy a coloring book together on the next visit. Then mail your grandchild a page from the coloring book every week. Toddlers love getting mail and will eagerly color in the picture to send it back to you.

Be there when you can: If you live nearby (or if not but you have vacation time available) go to an event for your grandkids (maybe instead of their parents). Take them to a toddler gym class or attend a preschool function. Your grandchild will love showing you around and showing you off.

Keep up on your grandchild's life: Watch one of their favorite shows on TV, then call them that day to talk about it.

310

Craft Projects

Make leis: Make a backyard barbecue more festive with Hawaiian leis. Flatten various-colored paper muffin cups and cut different petal shapes into them; you can even glue construction paper circles on for flower centers and leaves. Use a hole punch to make holes, and string them in small groups onto yarn, a shoelace, or string. Use dried pasta spacers in between the bunches.

Pet rocks: Go rock hunting and gather large and small rocks. If you'd like to hot glue them together, you can make animal bodies or just paint the flat rocks. Paint faces on them—don't forget hair, teeth, moustaches, and beards! Make sure Grandma and Grandpa make pets of their own.

311

Share Memories

Memories are the basics of family history. Help your grandchild build a concept of the past by sharing your memories of his parents as well as of your childhood.

* Share photos—and stories about the photos—of your grandkids' parents and yourselves as kids.
* Bring out the old awards, yearbooks, and autograph books from school. Talk about the memories they trigger.
* Talk about how you met your spouse, and what your children (their parents) looked and acted like when they were small (and how it compares to your grandkids).
* Share recipes. Cook your favorite recipes together. As you make them, talk about how your parents and grandparents made them with you.
* Encourage them to learn about their heritage. Teach them to count in the language of your ancestry, and show them where the family is from on a world map.

312

Start a Notebook

Grandparents see their grandchild differently than parents see him. While parents are busy with the job of disciplining and worrying if he is going to turn out morally sound, grandparents are enjoying every little thing. Start a notebook of remembrances and thoughts about your grandchild: how he is being raised, what you see him learning, the daily things he does while he's visiting you, favorite toys, funny sayings, or anything else that strikes your fancy. Make copies of the pages you write and give them to the parents. Your appreciation will shine through and perhaps shed new light on their child. This will be a treasured gift one day.

Words of Wisdom: *All I have to do to keep my grandkids entertained in the car is to bring a big colorful stopwatch. They love to compete and time themselves or guess how long it is going to take to get somewhere.*

—Elizabeth, Hudson, Wisconsin

313

Do the Unexpected

When the kids are with you, do something spontaneous and fun. But don't ever tell them it's a secret or to not tell their parents about it—that can be confusing for children of this age. Here are some ideas:

* Hide treats around the house during the visit—under a pillow, in folded socks, or anywhere. They will find the treats unexpectedly.
* Have snack baggies with fun treats waiting in the backseat for car rides.
* Show up to breakfast with temporary tattoos (available at drug and beauty supply stores) on your arms—and then give the kids coordinating ones.
* Make crazy hats. Start with plain hats (inexpensive ones can be bought at party stores—straw hats, top hats, etc.) and decorate together by gluing on feathers, boas, handkerchiefs, rope, etc. If you're really daring, wear them on errands or to the park!
* Host a kids' movie marathon one morning in your pajamas.

314

Spoiling

Spoiling your grandkids is half the fun of graduating to the role of grandparent. Just remember a few things:

- Don't overshadow parent gifts—you don't want the parents or Santa to feel like they can't compete with you.
- You may want to ask before giving something meaningful like a first doll, cradle, or first tricycle. The parents may be planning to give that themselves at a special time.
- Consider buying toys to keep at your house, especially the bigger things like tricycles, blocks, or a playhouse.
- Don't go overboard, especially when the kids are young and happy with almost anything you would give them. Something as small as a spinning top, a coloring book, or a pack of play dough will do.
- Think about opening a savings account or buying stock in something representative of your grandkids like a toy company.
- Give baby-sitting coupons. This will be a parent's favorite gift!

315

Family Totem Pole

This is a fun way to create something that represents each person as well as the family as a whole. Use various-sized cylinders or boxes, oatmeal containers, or other things that will stack on top of each other to resemble a totem pole. If you can, use a different shape for each family member. Give one to each child along with some magazines, old cards, family photos, glue, crayons, pens, paints, and construction paper. Help them to decorate the boxes and cylinders with things that represent who they are, including words that describe them, pictures doing things they like to do, as well as family pictures. When everyone is finished, erect the totem pole by firmly taping the sections together, one atop the other. If it's top-heavy, place a rock inside the bottom box to prevent the totem pole from toppling over.

316

Childproofing Grandma's House

Having the grandkids visit can be a challenge if you are unprepared. Make sure to have one child gate, ten electric outlet plugs, a roll of thick masking tape, rubber bands, and padded corner guards.

Before the arrival of the grandkids:

* Go through the house and take any cleaning supplies or poisonous products and put them out of reach.
* Scan the kitchen for appliances with cords within reach, move them to the back of counters, and masking tape the cords out of reach.
* Masking tape all cords around the house to the walls to make sure they are out of pulling reach.
* Remove tablecloths so kids won't pull any hot food or heavy items on top of themselves.
* Tape a sign to the bathroom mirrors as a reminder to keep doors closed at all times.
* Move beds and furniture away from the windows.
* Clear bedside tables.
* Move houseplants out of reach.
* Move low tables with sharp corners into closets or attach corner guards.
* Put rubber bands on the handles of any cabinets that are unsafe for kids to open.

317

Dream Supporter

As a grandparent and experienced parent, you can offer your child, who is now the parent in charge, perspective and wisdom. But don't make the mistake of pushing your ideas or expecting your child to do things as you did—things are different, just as you raised your children differently than your mom did. You've probably noticed things like potty-training and manners were emphasized at a much younger age when you raised your children. Pick up a parenting magazine at the newsstand to see the kinds of things your grandkids' parents are thinking about and doing. Know when to share your thoughts (without judging) and when to bite your tongue. Listen to your child's idea of what he or she thinks the right thing to do might be. Part of gaining confidence as a parent is learning to listen to your own voice. And don't forget to praise your child for all the great things he or she does for your grandkids!

318

Seasonal Fun

Flowers in Bloom

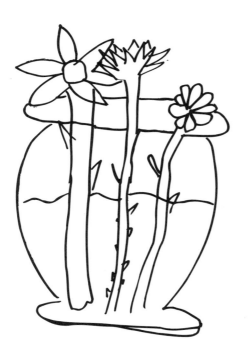

Age Range: 15 months and up

Take a walk around the garden in summer or go on a field trip to a nursery to see all the different kinds of flowers in bloom. Bring a sketch pad with you so you can draw your favorites to remind yourself what they look like. When you return home, make your own flowers in bloom with coffee filters, an eyedropper, food coloring, and green pipe cleaners for stems. Drop the food coloring onto the filters and then spray them with water. Watch the color spread. Cut the edges of filters if you want them to look more like petals. Pinch the center of the filter together and twist on a green pipe cleaner.

319

Tissue-Paper Egg

Age Range: 18 months and up

Eggs are a sign of new life in the springtime. Cut a large oval out of a piece of cardboard. Cut multiple colors of tissue paper into four-inch squares. Show your toddler how to crunch the tissue paper into balls. Dip the tissue paper balls into glue and attach them to the cardboard egg. You may want to draw a design on the cardboard in advance to include specific shapes, stripes, or your child's name. When finished, take a walk outside and look for birds' nests and point out how they might have eggs in them. Go to a pet store or petting zoo to see if they have any chicks hatching, or get a book with good pictures of bird development inside the egg.

320

Bouncy Bunnies

Age Range: 18 months and up

Materials
Construction paper or craft foam
Pipe cleaners
Cotton balls
Twelve-inch–square bulletin board

Cut out construction-paper bunnies and let the child decorate them with markers, crayons, and stickers. Or cut out craft-foam bunnies and glue on decorations. Don't forget to have them glue on a cotton-ball tail! Wrap pipe cleaners around a pencil to create a spring. Tape or glue (use hot glue for a strong hold) one end of each spring to a bunny and wrap the other end around a pushpin before pinning it to the bulletin board. The bunnies will bounce around at the slightest breeze! Kids love blowing on them, too. You can also attach them to the refrigerator using packing tape, and they will hop around whenever you open or close the door! This works great with frog and butterfly shapes as well.

321

Leaf Play

Age Range: 18 months and up

* Have your toddler help you rake up fall leaves. Get her a small children's rake so she can work alongside you.
* Let her crunch the leaves under her feet, run and jump into the piles you've made, or throw the leaves overhead and try to catch them.
* Put a big carton (large enough to hold her) underneath the leaf pile to create an "underground" playhouse.
* String leaves on laces or ribbons for a garland effect and hang them in the window or wear them as a necklace.
* Collect colorful leaves, remove the stems, and then crush them. Cut leaf shapes out of construction paper. Sponge on a thin layer of glue. Decorate with the fall leaf confetti you made.

322

Seasonal Treats

Age Range: 21 months and up

Winter: Make fresh snow cones with real snow and flavored syrups (syrups can be found at coffee shops, import stores, big all-purpose stores, and many grocery stores).

Spring: To liven up and beautify a springtime salad, add a few edible flowers—pansies, violas, marigold petals, honeysuckle, lilac, dandelions, nasturtiums, peach and pear blossoms, queen Anne's lace, tulip petals, or rose petals. Use only petals on most flowers and be sure they weren't in contact with any pesticides. Rinse for bugs before eating.

Summer: Make graham-cracker and frozen-yogurt sandwiches. Sun s'mores are also fun. Put chocolate chips and minimarshmallows on top of a graham cracker placed in a foil pie plate and covered in foil. Leave them in the sun for about ten minutes until melted.

Fall: Slice up apples. Peel caramels and melt them. Drizzle the caramel over the apple slices.

323

Pumpkin Head

Age Range: 21 months and up

When you're searching for a pumpkin-decorating method that toddlers can actually do themselves, try making this pumpkin head. Gather all the Mr., Mrs., or Baby Potato Head pieces you have. Set the pumpkin on the table surrounded by various eyes, noses, mouths, ears, mustaches, and hats. Mom or Dad needs to poke a small hole into the pumpkin where facial features should be. Then let your toddler try out all sorts of different combinations until he finds one he likes. You might want to keep the potato head supplies in a bowl so that your child can change the face each day until the pumpkin needs to be thrown out.

324

Snow Fun

Age Range: 24 months and up

Snow pictures: Fill a spray bottle with water and food coloring. Find a smooth patch of snow and spray the colored water until you create a masterpiece.

Angel bird feeder: Make an angel in the snow by lying on top of a flat patch of snow and moving your arms and legs back and forth. Get up without making footprints in the angel. Use corn kernels, seeds, wild birdseed, cranberries, or other food birds will eat to make a design within the angel. Sit back and watch the birds enjoy your creation.

Snowflake catcher: Take two pieces of black velvet, felt, or material and sew three sides together. Stick a piece of cardboard or plastic inside and then sew it up. Sew a string with a cheap magnifying glass to the fabric square. It also works to paint a piece of cardboard black. Take it outside, let the snow fall upon it and examine flakes with the magnifying glass.

Indoor wonderland: When it's too cold to go out and play in the snow, collect it in big buckets and play with it in the bathtub.

325

Seasonal Journals

Age Range: 24 months and up

At the beginning of each new season, buy an instant camera to document the progression of nature as it blooms or fades. Take one picture every other day for two months. Write a note in the journal describing what you've photographed on the day you take each picture. You'll also want to remember what the weather was like, any animals you might have seen, how you were feeling, or what your child was doing. When the pictures are developed, glue them into the journal on the appropriate pages. Make sure your child is in some of the pictures dressed accordingly; they are fun to look back on as the seasons and years go by.

326

Ice Melt

Age Range: 30 to 36 months

Salt when placed on ice will melt the ice and create intricate designs. Freeze water in an empty milk carton to create an ice block. When the ice is solid, tear off the cardboard. Place the ice block on a tray covered with several layers of newspaper. Have your child sprinkle the coarse rock salt on top of the ice block and then drip various colors of food coloring on top of the ice block. You'll see cool tunnels of color created as the salt melts through the ice and the colored water seeps in.

....

Words of Wisdom: *To keep our son busy on Christmas morning while other family members open presents, I wrap up a bunch of empty boxes and let him unwrap those.*
—Amy, Dallas, North Carolina

327

Kiddy Pool Games

Age Range: 30 to 36 months

The backyard baby pool is a source of great fun all summer long.
Concentration: Cut flat household sponges into three-inch squares. Cut pairs of shapes—two hearts, two stars, etc.—from foam sheets. Hot glue a shape to one side of each sponge. Place them all in the water and have your child match them up.

Target practice: Float an upside-down Frisbee or plastic ring on top of the water. Have kids toss sponges to see if they can hit the target.

Will it float? guessing game: Fill a bowl or box with all sorts of items: a whole orange, a slice of orange, a balloon, a piece of lettuce, a quarter, a rock, or anything else you find interesting. Before putting each item in the pool, let your child guess whether or not it will float.

Water transfer game: Scoop water from a bucket to the pool and back with a cup. Try doing it with a turkey baster. Set a kitchen buzzer and count how many cups you can scoop out of the pool in five minutes.

328

Sugar Cube Igloo

Age Range: 30 to 36 months

Materials
Cardboard
Popsicle sticks (optional)
Large sugar cubes
Homemade or store-bought white icing
Gummy penguins (optional)

Draw a four- to six-inch circle on a piece of cardboard. With fingers or Popsicle sticks, spread icing along the circle. Put the sugar cubes around the circle on top of the icing, pressing them into the cardboard. Carefully spread the icing on top of the first row of sugar cubes and stack a smaller ring of cardboard on top. Repeat this process until you have an igloo. Get creative and see if you can construct an arched doorway. Gummy penguins complete the package!

329

Weather Board

Age Range: 36 months and up

Help your child be more aware of the weather around her as the seasons come and go. This activity is best to do at a time of year when the weather will not be the same day after day. Mount seven squares of felt, one for each day of the week, onto a larger sheet of felt. Then cut out a bunch of felt weather symbols: a sun, a sun with a cloud over it, a cloud with raindrops, a snowflake, or any other weather possibilities in your area. At the same time each day of the week, have your child select the appropriate symbol to reflect the day's weather. You can also play a guessing game where you guess what the weather will be like the next day. Sit with your child when the weather forecaster appears on the nightly news, show her the pictures of the clouds moving over the earth, and explain how there are all sorts of ways to predict the weather.

330

Homemade Cards

Age Range: 24 months and up

Handprint wreath cards: Use green finger paints to make holiday-wreath cards. Have the child "stamp" her hand all the way around in a circle (wrists to the center of the circle, fingers fanning out), forming the boughs of the wreath. Paint or attach a red bow.

Pencil toppers: You'll need craft foam, permanent markers, and pipe cleaners. Cut the craft foam into a heart, shamrock, egg, balloon, or other appropriate holiday shape. Write a message on the shape. Poke the pipe cleaner through the foam to attach. Have your child wrap the pipe cleaner around a pencil to make a kind of spring. Pull the sponge up about an inch so it bobs above the pencil.

· ·

Words of Wisdom: *Each holiday season my kids and I enjoy making recycled cards. We save holiday cards from the year before, cut off the front of each card, and glue it onto construction paper folded in half like a card. Then we write a new holiday message inside.*

—Ursela, Port Washington, Wisconsin

Section Five:
Growing and Learning

Recording Your Thoughts

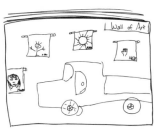

Art Storage Ideas

- Before storing your child's favorite artwork, ask him to tell you about each piece as you record his response on cassette tape. When finished, date and label the tape and store it with the piece of art.
- Keep one or two pieces of artwork from each month of the year and glue them into last year's calendar—it's almost like a yearly portfolio.
- Videotape your child next to his piece of artwork; that way you'll see how old your child was when he created it as well as hear a description in his own voice.
- Display artwork on the walls of your garage. That way you can see it each morning when you leave the house, and it will give the dull garage walls a little life.

332

Books on Tape

Whenever you read a storybook to your child, record yourself. You will also catch your child's voice on the tape asking questions or pointing out something he likes about the story. Then attach the tape to the back of the book in an envelope so your child can listen to it when you are gone or busy. Make sure to record yourself when you sing songs together, too!

Words of Wisdom: *Always write a note in the books you give your child. Talk about why you selected it, and why she deserves it. Don't forget to add the date.*

—Richard, Level Green, Pennsylvania

333

Birthday Memories

* Each year on your child's birthday, videotape him doing his usual daily activities. Show him eating his favorite breakfast, playing with toys and out in the yard with pets, taking a bath, doing his chores, or whatever else he would do that day. Also record parts of his birthday party. Store this special tape to be pulled out each year on his birthday. When you give him this tape on his eighteenth birthday or when he leaves home, he'll have a wonderful record (all on one tape) of how he spent the everyday moments of his life.
* Sit down and draft a letter to your child on the eve of every birthday. Talk about what he's like, what he's accomplished, and what joy he brings you.

334

Everyday Things

- Thank-you notes: Write little notes to your child thanking her for ordinary things, like taking turns at a game or being good at a restaurant.
- Compliment your child often and let him overhear you bragging about him to someone else.
- Read the paper (hand over the comics!) and have a cup of coffee (or milk!) with your child.
- Sit together and chitchat on a regular basis.
- Use loving nicknames that make everyone smile.
- Whenever you can, live life on toddler time.

••

Words of Wisdom: *One day I found my daughter covered, head to toe, in flour. She'd gotten into the baking cupboard. Instead of capturing the hilarious sight on film, I immediately swooped in and cleaned her and the kitchen up. I regret not snapping a photo first. My new motto: shoot first, then clean (or punish, as the case may be!). Those memories can't be re-created!*

—Jean, Fairport, New York

335

Guest Book

Buy or make a guest book for your child's room. Invite visitors to write little notes, hopes, and remembrances. Periodically have your child write in it to record his handwriting and drawing abilities as they evolve. Take a photograph of your child with each guest and add it to the book next to the guest's note or signature. As years pass the same guests will most likely visit, so you'll have a photographic record over time.

··

Words of Wisdom: *I have started to keep a small journal where I make notes about when we have had really great behavior days. It's good to review on more difficult days!*
—Carrie, Wichita, Kansas

336

Say Cheese!

Follow these tips for great photographs:

- Don't be stingy with film. Snap away—it will be worth the expense to get those perfect shots!
- Select places with simple backgrounds (or create plain backdrops—a drop cloth, a sheet, etc.) and, if possible, natural lighting (bright but overcast days are ideal for outdoor shooting).
- Try to look for natural "frames" for the composition (a tree branch, an archway or doorway, even a stroller canopy), and watch out for unintended distractions (dark shadows, a pole that might appear to be coming out of your child's head).
- Enlist the help of an animated partner to entertain the child while you're behind the camera.
- If you have a zoom feature on your camera, use it to get close instead of getting the camera in the face of your child, which may make him self-conscious.
- Consider using black-and-white film for a classic, artsy shoot.
- Don't pose children—wait for them to get engrossed in something and capture that spirit.
- Get on eye level with the child for a true-to-life perspective.
- If there is more than one live subject (child and a parent, another child, or a pet), encourage them to engage with and touch one another.

Through the Years

Even though you spend every day with your child, you may find yourself absent from most photos years down the road. To avoid being asked, "Where were you?" make sure to jump in front of the camera once in a while. For the first year or two you may want to do a photo shoot every few months, and after that every six months to a year will work. Make sure to take the photo in the same position—for example, the child standing in front of or beside her parent. That way you'll see the evolution of both! Create a special scrapbook just for these portraits. While you are taking this photo, make sure to ask the photographer to take some silly ones of the two of you hugging, laughing, throwing a ball, or making faces. You can put these alongside the portrait in a sequence of events shot.

338

Jolly St. Nick

Make an ongoing list of what Santa brings your child every year, as well as what she asks for, which is sometimes hilarious! Save letters to Santa, birthday lists, or any other requests your child makes for gifts. When she's all grown up and complaining how much stuff her own kids have and want, you can pull out her own not-so-little lists for a stroll down memory lane.

Words of Wisdom: *My son always froze in front of the video camera, so we could never capture whatever charming thing he was doing. We have the kind with the tiny swivel screen in addition to the eyepiece. Once we started using the eyepiece for filming and swiveling the screen so that he could watch himself as we taped, he really got into it!*

—Matt, Tallahassee, Florida

339

Silhouettes

Use masking tape to affix dark construction paper to a smooth wall. Turn on a light source: a slide-show projector, flashlight, or lamp. Place your child standing sideways in front of construction paper so that you get a profile image of his face on the paper. You might have to move the light source closer or farther back to make it fit on the paper. Trace your child's profile with white chalk. Remove the paper from the wall. Cut out the profile and glue it onto light-colored construction paper. Write the child's name, age, and date on it. If you do one of these every year, take the current year's silhouette and move it to the back of the frame. At some point you may want to move them to a larger frame and put all the past silhouettes in a yearly progression.

340

Storybook

Use your child's artwork to make a storybook. Be sure to have your child tell you about the art as soon as it comes in the door or leaves the drawing table. Jot down the story behind it, the characters involved, and what is going on in the picture. Write or type the story on a separate piece of paper and then glue it to the back of the picture. Keep them in a box or tie them together by punching holes in the top and tying with yarn. If you want to make a longer story by putting many pictures together, try to pick artwork with similar themes and then create a story using the pictures.

341

Scrapbook Flare

A child or family scrapbook can be so much more than an attractive colorful layout of photos with a cute headline. The most vital element in a scrapbook is narration—personal reflections on who is in the photographs and thoughts on when, where, and why the event took place. Most parents remember to document vacations, holidays, and birthdays, but to really capture life with your toddler, consider some everyday themes.

* How many times have you looked at old family photos and zoomed in on the background for clues about how the subjects lived? Make those things intentional in your scrapbook so your child can one day laugh with her grandchildren about the kinds of cars you drive, the home she grew up in and its furniture, or the clothes she wore.
* Use the nicknames you call your toddler—and tell the story behind them.
* Document the hilarious things she says and does.
* Focus on her favorites—stories, hobbies, and foods. Maybe even write about what she adamantly *doesn't* like.
* On birthdays, capture more than just the traditional candle-blowing, cake-eating, and present-opening shots; write about who she is, what she might become given what you know about her (is she so convincing and outspoken that she has lawyer potential?) and your hopes for her.

Your Child's Journal

Buy a blank book and start writing to your child today. Your child may not be born or your child may be two years old; whatever the age, it is never too late to begin recording your thoughts, feelings, observations, and descriptions of your child's life and personality. Write as often as you can and include your feelings about your baby, how she contributes to the beauty of your life, and most of all your feelings of love. Write letters to her, things you want her to know when she is an adult, cute things she does that you might forget over time. As she grows into adolescence, read her some of your thoughts when she is going through a hard time or when she thinks you hate her because you need to correct a behavior. It will remind her that you have been loving her for a very long time. When your child leaves home, give her this precious journal. This might just be the gift she will cherish most from you.

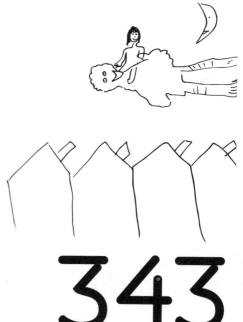

343

12 Games
Parents Play

Baby Daycare

New Twist to Reward Charts

Younger children often don't see the benefit of the sticker system as a reward for good behavior or potty training. Here are a few options to try:

* Take a large poster of his favorite character. Glue it onto a piece of cardboard and cut it out into a simple puzzle. Each successful potty trip or good behavior results in adding a new piece to the puzzle. When the puzzle is complete, he gets a prize.
* If your child is into trains, draw up a train track. Each successful potty trip (or whatever) gets a sticker—and one track closer to the end prize…a new train!
* You can do the same with an ice-cream cone—fill in all the waffle diamonds and the child gets a trip to an ice-cream parlor!

344

Separation Anxiety

Make a photo album for your child to take along to daycare, pre-school, or the baby-sitter. Place a photo of a family member on one side with a small bio or interesting tale written on the other. This will help the caregiver to know about the child's loved ones, house, or favorite toys so that she can relate to the child on a familiar level. In addition, it's a great icebreaker for the child!

Words of Wisdom: *We wanted the transition to day care to be as smooth as possible. When we'd selected a place, we brought our son there to visit a few times before his first day. We had him pose for a cheerful photo with each of his new caregivers. Then we displayed the photos in his room and talked about them often—pointing out the friendly smiles of the caregivers, the bright colors in the background, the neat race-car rug underneath them, etc. That way he felt much more familiar and comfortable on his first day.*

—Ashley, Huntsville, Alabama

345

Aggression

Hitting, biting, and hair-pulling are common behaviors for toddlers. Be firm that these behaviors aren't tolerated. Say "No!" and remove your child from the situation immediately and matter-of-factly. Don't give him any extra attention (even negative); instead lavish the attention on the injured party. That way there's no reward for the aggressive behavior, so it's likely to stop, given time. Teach your child to say that he's sorry, and require that he help soothe the person he hurt. This will help him realize the pain he caused and become more compassionate and nurturing (also, of course, over time!).

Words of Wisdom: *I've learned I have to pick my battles. I let my son make choices in the little things like what he wants to wear or eat. That way when I need to make a choice, he usually goes along with it.*

—Gill, Columbus, Georgia

346

Boredom Busters

When all the toys seem suddenly boring, here are a few tricks to have up your sleeve:

* Get into the habit of rotating toys. Every month, put a bunch of them in a box or laundry basket to be stored out in the garage where your child won't see them.
* Create theme boxes. Fill a box with a particular theme and pull it out when the need arises. For example, collect hair items for a hairdresser box, stickers for a sticker box, play-dough toys with some tubs of play dough, various-sized containers for sorting pasta pieces, old telephone and other office supplies for an "office box," a dress-up box, or block-building box. When organized like this, the activities will be easier to facilitate and won't require your full participation.

347

Potty-Training Readiness

Don't panic if your child is slow to be potty trained. Rest assured he will not be wearing diapers when he enters kindergarten! You'll know your child is ready to give potty training a try when you see the following signs:

- He expresses interest by watching Mom and Dad and maybe even sitting on the toilet himself.
- He understands what the toilet is for and knows the words for going potty.
- He can stay dry for a couple of hours at a time.
- He seems to recognize having a bowel movement—he squats, makes "the look," etc.
- He would rather not be wearing diapers and is interested in big-boy pants.

348

Tooth Brushing Basics

- Do it regularly—never give up. Floss, too, if you can.
- Use only a pea-sized amount of toothpaste and encourage him to spit, not swallow.
- Brush alongside him so he can mimic you, but always follow up by brushing his teeth yourself!
- If he can't see into the mirror, set a small stand-up mirror on the bathroom counter so he can see.
- Let him brush your teeth.
- For fun, turn off the bathroom light and shine a flashlight on his teeth while your child looks into a mirror and brushes.
- Have him brush a favorite puppet or stuffed animal for practice. Have a stuffed animal "hold" the brush. Let him choose his own toothbrush and toothpaste.

349

Picky Eaters

- Keep a bowl of healthy snacks in either the refrigerator or cupboard that is within your child's reach or view. Bag up trail mixes, Cheerios, or other snacks that you don't mind her eating, and let her choose from the bowl when she is hungry. The ability to choose for herself often appeals to a toddler's need for authority and gets your child eating when her normally picky little mind might refrain.
- Surprise her with unexpected combinations. Serve breakfast for dinner, use flat-bottomed ice-cream cones as food cups with yogurt or cottage cheese inside, or be artistic with food presentation using cookie cutters to shape sandwiches or making funny faces or scenes out of the food.
- Have her participate in cooking and even vegetable gardening!
- Kids love to dip—offer healthy dips such as mild salsas, yogurt, cottage cheese, cream cheese, guacamole, and pureed fruits.
- Serve smoothies. These can be made out of yogurt, fruit juice, ice cubes, or sherbet, with fresh fruit. Freeze the fresh fruit in advance if you don't want to use ice or sherbet.

350

Positive Naptime

Toddlers like choices and negotiation, so it helps to offer your child naptime options, such as, "Would you like your curtains open or closed?" or "Which animal would you like to nap with?" But don't offer him the option not to nap, as he needs a regular break from activity as much as you do. If he doesn't want to nap, make him a deal. Go through the usual naptime routine, but assure him that it's fine if he chooses not to sleep. He can play with his animals or whatever he likes. The only rule is that he has to do it in the crib or bed in his own room. That way, you'll both achieve the much-needed downtime. You may find that after he plays quietly for a while, your child will doze off despite his intentions to stay up and play. Establish a pattern of naptime or quiet time every afternoon at least until your child begins first grade.

351

Kicking the Pacifier

It's best to eliminate the pacifier somewhere between the ages of two and five. The sooner the better, say many dentists, pediatricians, and speech therapists. The best way to start is with daytime elimination. Keep the pacifier out of reach and out of sight or at least inconvenient, so your child has to request it. This will make sucking it a conscious decision versus a mindless habit. Try to replace it with something soothing, such as humming. Start humming around her whenever she is sucking on her pacifier. Give her some control in the process by setting up a token system. You begin by giving her five tokens to trade, each worth fifteen minutes of daytime pacifier use. As time goes on, you can give her fewer tokens per day.

352

Transfer to Big-Kid Bed

This is a big deal in the life of a toddler. For some, the idea is a wonderful adventure. Then there are others who are very reluctant to give up the safety and familiarity of the crib. Here are a few tips to make the transition a success:

- Put the new bed against the wall and a detachable guardrail on the outside. This leaves fewer ways for your child to fall out of bed.
- Take your child to the store to buy the bed, new sheets, and bedspread. Once he sees all the fun character sheets, he'll be excited about his new bed décor.
- At first you might want to put the crib or twin mattress on the floor. That will quiet the fear of falling out of bed.
- If the move to a big bed is required because a new baby is on the way, make the switch at least two months before the new baby arrives. Otherwise your toddler is going to feel like he was kicked out of his bed.
- For safety reasons, you need to make a transition to a bed when your child is able to climb out of the crib or is thirty-five inches tall, whichever happens first.

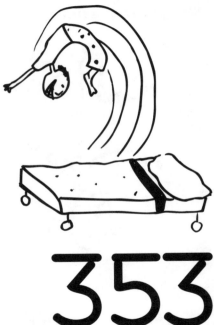

353

Thumb-Be-Gone

Most dentists would like toddlers to stop sucking their thumbs by age three. But the problem with a thumb is that it is always handy. You can't take it away, keep it out of reach, or trade it in for something else. Here's what you can do:

❋ Keep your toddlers hands busy by offering her a toy to hold when she'd rather be sucking her thumb. Maybe she could stroke or twirl her doll's hair or rub her hand on a smooth rock.

❋ Buy fun Band-Aids, or make your own by putting stickers on top of plain ones. Let her choose which one to put on her thumb each morning.

❋ Have her wear mittens or socks on her hands at night.

❋ Try the bitter substance that is made to prevent thumb-sucking that you paint on, but let her paint it on so she feels in control.

❋ Reward little steps toward success. If she doesn't suck her thumb for an hour, she gets a sticker or treat. The goal is to lessen the amount of time she needs to suck her thumb, gradually replacing it with other self-soothing techniques.

354

Dawdler Toddler

Most toddlers dawdle at some point during the day, often at mealtime, bedtime, and anytime you're in a big hurry to get somewhere. Here's what you can do to speed them up:

* Make a game of the activity by challenging her to a race: "I wonder who can get her socks on the fastest?"
* Set a timer or count to ten. Usually the excitement of the countdown motivates.
* Move her away from distractions like TV and toys.
* Be sure to give her enough time to accomplish things in her own time and at her skill level.
* Maintain schedules and routines that help her to anticipate when she needs to do things. Take your afternoon trip to the park as soon as she wakes up from her nap so she knows she needs to get ready to go.
* Remind her of any inherent rewards for getting something done faster—more time at the park if you leave now or another quick story before bed if she gets her teeth brushed.
* Praise her when she does accomplish something efficiently.

355

Fifteen to Eighteen Months— Do and Feel

Physically, your toddler may:

- Walk without support
- Untie shoes
- Bowl over other children or pets with exuberance and lack of coordination
- Eat smaller meals, but snack often
- Stack two to three blocks

Emotionally, your toddler may:

- Express a variety of feelings
- Be unpredictable
- Respond to others' emotions and expressions
- Show preferences for toys and people
- Become easily frustrated
- Start to display temper tantrums

356

Development

Fifteen to Eighteen Months– Express and Think

Socially, your toddler may:
* Have difficulty sharing toys and attention
* Show affection
* Demand attention from caregivers
* Be wary of unfamiliar faces and places
* Express fear of things like loud noises and large animals

Intellectually, your toddler may:
* Follow simple requests
* Find things that are hidden
* Use trial and error to figure things out
* Use physical gestures to communicate
* Know and use a handful of simple words (including "no")
* Realize words stand for things
* Imitate animal sounds

357

Eighteen to Twenty-One Months— Do and Feel

Physically, your toddler may:
- Walk confidently
- Try running and climbing
- Attempt to walk up stairs with help
- Feed herself (albeit sloppily!)
- Scribble with crayon or marker
- Stack several blocks
- Drink from a cup
- Unzip zippers

Emotionally, your toddler may:
- Mimic emotional expressions
- Be dependent upon a security object like a pacifier, stuffed animal, or blanket
- Become angry at a cause of frustration
- Show frequent temper tantrums

358

Eighteen to Twenty-One Months– Express and Think

Socially, your toddler may:
* Begin to express sympathy
* Reveal feelings of jealousy
* Sometimes cooperate
* Enjoy being with other children (but will not yet interact with them)
* Imitate other children and adults
* Be trusting of adults

Intellectually, your toddler may:
* Understand "mine"
* Eagerly help with simple household tasks
* Engage in imaginative play
* Enjoy brief, simple games
* Be very curious, but have a short attention span
* Name familiar objects and people

359

Twenty-One to Twenty-Four Months— Do and Feel

Physically, your toddler may:
- Walk quickly (and maybe even walk backwards)
- Become more adept at running and climbing (possibly out of the crib!)
- Walk up stairs
- Begin having bladder and bowel control
- Enjoy trying to dress and undress herself
- Show aggression, such as hitting, pushing, or biting
- Often dawdle
- Enjoy activities like digging, playing with and in water, and dancing to music

Emotionally, your toddler may:
- Openly express love
- Be easily hurt by criticism
- Fear disapproval or rejection
- Have rapid and intense mood shifts

360

Twenty-One to Twenty-Four Months– Express and Think

Socially, your toddler may:
- Engage in simple fantasy play
- Be increasingly possessive of toys and caregivers
- Desire to please caregivers
- Enjoy playmates

Intellectually, your toddler may:
- Think problems through before taking action
- Use growing vocabulary to get attention and needs met
- Use own name in reference to self
- Speak two- and three-word sentences

361

Twenty-Four to Thirty Months–Do and Feel

Physically, your toddler may:
- Walk down stairs
- Run smoothly, but still be working on stopping and turning
- Throw and kick a ball
- Attempt jumping with both feet (though rarely get much air!)
- Stand on tiptoes
- Eat with utensils and spill less often
- Dress herself in simple clothing
- Use a paintbrush and build block towers
- Wash and dry hands
- Possibly show interest and take strides in potty training

Emotionally, your toddler may:
- Feel and express pride in accomplishments
- Crave immediate gratification
- Express fear of the dark
- Assert "no" frequently and adamantly

362

Twenty-Four to Thirty Months—Express and Think

Socially, your toddler may:
* Waffle between striving for independence and needing caregiver assurance and security
* Display difficulty sharing
* Grab toys from other children
* Be sometimes willing to trade toys

Intellectually, your toddler may:
* Be able to name body parts
* Work large-piece puzzles
* Narrate what she is doing as she does it
* Like to take things apart and put them back together (such as screwing lids on jars)
* Follow and begin to carry on a simple conversation

363

Thirty to Thirty-Six Months– Do and Feel

Physically, your toddler may:
* Like to hide
* Enjoy tumbling
* Refuse help with tasks
* Love to do household chores
* Pedal a tricycle
* Make more deliberate strokes with crayon or marker (circular shapes, lines, etc.)
* Briefly balance on one foot

Emotionally, your toddler may:
* Display the occasional temper
* Thrive on the security and comfort of routines
* Express affection openly and easily
* Separate more easily from parents

364

Thirty to Thirty-Six Months-Express and Think

Socially, your toddler may:
* Understand "mine" and "yours"
* Have a little less difficulty sharing
* Prefer doing things by herself and expect praise afterward
* Enjoy other children and begin playing with them instead of alongside them
* Engage in cooperative play
* Begin to take turns

Intellectually, your toddler may:
* Become skilled at problem-solving
* Understand make-believe play
* Recognize and identify most familiar objects and people
* Understand most sentences and requests
* Grasp physical relationships ("in," "under," etc.)
* Use "I," "me," "you," and plurals but not always correctly
* Be understood by strangers
* Distinguish between boys and girls
* Join in simple songs and rhymes
* Match objects to pictures and sort objects by shape and color

365

Sources

American Academy of Pediatrics, *Caring for Your Baby and Young Child: Birth to Age 5,* New York: Bantam 1998.

Arlene Eisenberg, Heidi E. Murkoff, and Sandee E. Hathaway, B.S.N., *What to Expect: The Toddler Years,* New York: Workman 1996.

Tracy Hogg and Melinda Blau, *Secrets of the Baby Whisperer for Toddlers*, New York: Ballantine Books 2003.

Vicki Iovine, *The Girlfriends' Guide to Toddlers*, New York: Perigee 1999.

Linda Sonna, Ph.D., *The Everything Toddler Book*, Avon, Massachusettes: Adams Media Corporation 2002.

Richard C. Woolfson, *Bright Toddler: Understand and Stimulate Your Child's Development*, New York: Barron's Educational Series 2001.

http://www.babycenter.com

http://www.nncc.org (National Network for Childcare)

Special Thanks

A special thanks to Brigid Corboy, a very talented art teacher at Corte Madera School in Portola Valley, California, who organized the production of the imaginative illustrations produced by the following children:

Alex Piccolotti

Hannah Bourgeois

Lucy Rose Turner

Audrey Bullwinkel

Danielle De Broel

Danielle Knaak

Courtney Kubiak

Jennifer

Stephanie R. Chow

Madison

Alyssa Sontag

Ashley Evans

Eliza Turner

Beth Polack

Susan Berman

Christine Somersett

Laura Sisson

Taylor Hatfield

Kaitlin Carano

Charlotte Brown

Josephine Lihoff

Morgan Reinert

Christina Hajikham

Kelly O'Neill

Jon Schectman

Paige Reinert

Nicole Westly

Eric Fennel

Kelly Kubiak

Jennifer Nicole Thomas

Loren Virginia Conner

Eric Wegener

About the Author

Sheila Ellison is the dedicated mother of four children ages eighteen, seventeen, fourteen, and twelve, and the stepmother of two, ages seventeen and thirteen. She is the creator and author of the 365 Series of parenting books, including *365 Games Babies Play*, *365 Days of Creative Play*, *365 Afterschool Activities*, *365 Foods Kids Love to Eat*, and *365 Ways to Raise Great Kids*. She has appeared on *Oprah*, the *Later Today Show*, and the *CBS Early Show*. Her books have been featured in *O Magazine*, *Parenting*, *Family Circle*, *Glamour*, *Complete Woman*, *Healthy Kids Magazine*, *New York Daily News*, and *San Francisco Chronicle,* and have been selections of the Children's Book-of-the-Month Club. Sheila has appeared on hundreds of radio shows across the country. She continues to write and lives in Northern California.

Sheila Ellison's COMPLETE M♥M.com

Moms are busy people. We need fresh information right now about how to have fun with our kids, understand ourselves better, create strong relationships, enjoy our careers, and still have time to make cookies once in a while! Please visit me online at www.CompleteMom.com.

What you will find on the site:

* Parenting articles, advice, and ideas
* Activities to nurture Mom
* Creative, fun, and interactive activities for every age (including teens)
* Tasty time-tested recipes, party ideas, and games
* Ideas for building healthy relationships, igniting romance, and having great sex
* Women's health topics including exercise, stress release, and nutrition news
* A place to chat with other mothers on the extensive message boards
* A way to find the words to all your favorite childhood songs
* Contact Sheila
* AND MUCH MORE!